A SOLITARY SORROW

A Solitary Sorrow

Finding
Healing &
Wholeness
after
Abortion

Teri Reisser, M.S., M.F.T.
with Paul Reisser, M.D.

Foreword by Paul Meier, M.D.

HAROLD
SHAW
PUBLISHERS

Wheaton, Illinois

ISBN 0-87788-774-8

Cover design by Thomas Leo

Front cover photograph courtesy of Scott Barrow, Inc. SuperStock
Author photograph courtesy of Mark Brandes Studio

Library of Congress Cataloging-in-Publication Data

Reisser, Teri K.
    A solitary sorrow : finding healing and wholeness after abortion /
by Teri K. Reisser and Paul Reisser.
       p. cm.
    Includes bibliographical references.
    ISBN 0-87788-774-8
    1. Abortion—United States—Psychological aspects. 2. Abortion—
Religious aspects—Christianity. 3. Abortion counseling—United States.
4. Post-traumatic stress disorder. I. Reisser, Paul C. II. Title.

HQ767.5.U5 K453 1999
363.46—dc21   99-036846

04 03 02 01 00 99

10 9 8 7 6 5 4 3 2 1

*Dedicated to the hundreds of
post-abortion women who handed me
their tremulous hearts and trusted me
in an utterly vulnerable state.
Their healing is precious to me.*

❖ ❖ ❖

Contents

❖ ❖ ❖ ❖ ❖

Foreword   9

Acknowledgments   10

Introduction: Amanda's Story   11

Part One: The Silent Epidemic   **19**

Chapter One
  The Experience No One Talks About   21

Chapter Two
  No Longer Coping   48

Chapter Three
  Beginning to Grieve   75

Part Two: The Healing Journey   **87**

Chapter Four
  Facing the Past   89

Chapter Five
  Guilt and Forgiveness   101

Chapter Six
  Releasing the Anger   119

Chapter Seven
  Accepting the Loss   132

Chapter Eight
  Moving On   150

Appendix One
A Brief History of Post-Abortion Syndrome   168

Appendix Two
Journaling Exercise: Created for Love   180

Appendix Three
Teens and Abortion   184

Appendix Four
More for Friends, Men, Family, and Pastors   200

Appendix Five
Proposed Diagnostic Criteria for Post-Abortion
Syndrome   209

Appendix Six
Suggested Resources   213

Notes   217

Foreword

❖ ❖ ❖ ❖ ❖ ❖

As a psychiatrist, I have personally talked with many women (and a few men) who struggle with the emotional and psychological after-effects of abortion—post-abortion syndrome (PAS). That is why I am so excited that my friends Teri and Paul Reisser have so lovingly and accurately put together *A Solitary Sorrow*.

This is the best, most thorough, and most compassionate book I have ever read on post-abortion syndrome. It thoroughly and compassionately covers the facts about PAS, the stages, and how to bring about healing and recovery. It is a must read for every woman (or involved man) who has had an abortion or who is considering an abortion. The effects of PAS can be immediate or show up years later. This book will help women and men recognize the reality of post-abortion struggles and find healing. I highly recommend *A Solitary Sorrow* and plan to give away many copies of this book to my future patients.

Paul Meier, M.D.
Cofounder and Medical Director of the New Life Clinics nationally, and author of over forty books

Acknowledgments

❖ ❖ ❖ ❖ ❖ ❖

Angels of encouragement include Paul (who helped shape this book at the expense of missing the deadline for his own book project), Angie Côté (a new mommy who is also my training buddy and a great friend), Chad, Erica, and Carrie (my cheerleaders), and Elisa Fryling (the editor who put up with me).

Introduction:
Amanda's Story

❖ ❖ ❖ ❖ ❖ ❖

When it came to relationships with the opposite sex, Amanda had been a genuine "late bloomer." She was not outgoing enough to scale even the lower rungs of the pecking order in the seventh and eighth grades and had trouble finding a particular niche. She did have one good friend whose company became a port in the daily storm. Without Sara, she never would have made it through school.

While she was plodding through the first semester of the eighth grade, Amanda's parents decided to separate. Her mom worked hard to keep tabs on Amanda's feelings, which were not readily available for public inspection. Dad was not long in finding a condo and a new girlfriend. Despite eloquent promises that Amanda would always be his "best girl," the phone calls and visits began to dwindle and then disappeared altogether. For four years, Sara and Amanda kept each other afloat, fending off loneliness.

The summer before her senior year of high school, Amanda landed a small part in a teen musical, took more interest in cosmetics and clothing, and began to make up for lost time.

Daniel, a perennial in the Drama Club, began to talk with her—thoughtfully, pleasantly, and attentively. The two of them shared coffee and emotions began to stir. As they spent more time together, and as hand-holding and embraces shifted from secret thrills to casual openness, Amanda's mother began to issue warnings about "getting too serious." But Amanda found herself in a euphoric bubble. Her conversations with Daniel were plumbing new depths of intimacy and acceptance, the words "Together Forever" appeared inside her notebook, and finally their fervent embraces went much farther than she had ever expected.

Two months later, Amanda learned she was pregnant. *How could this have happened?* she wondered. *Daniel had always used a condom after our first time. Now what?* Amanda had a vague idea that abortion was wrong, especially after she had watched a TV documentary about the first weeks of human life. The images stuck with her. She knew that what was floating in her uterus wasn't just a late period waiting to be cut loose.

Daniel met her within the hour. He was amazingly calm and his comments were measured, as though he had rehearsed them for a play. He would be there for her but there was no way she should go through with a pregnancy. He had saved some money, and he knew a clinic that could take care of this problem. Next week was spring break, and he would even schedule the appointment. Daniel spelled out the dismal alternatives to ending the pregnancy. How would she face her mom? What would her father do? Who would pay the bills? She had always wanted to go to college, but she could kiss that good-bye in exchange for an endless trail of smelly diapers and sleepless nights.

It bothered Amanda that her lover hadn't painted himself into any of these gloomy scenarios. *He wouldn't walk out on me like Dad did. . . . would he?* she thought. She became more irritable and depressed as she realized that his deliberations ignored the fact that this baby had come from both of them. *He just wants me fixed.*

Amanda was certain that her dearest friend, Sara, would understand why she didn't want an abortion and would hear her out. But Sara sang the same refrain about parents and college and bills, and even added a cutting remark about the possibility that Daniel's eyes would begin to wander when Amanda's bikini no longer fit. And so Amanda called Daniel, and Daniel called the clinic, and the following week the two of them drove in silence across town, in the opposite direction from the beach where she had told her mom they would be spending the afternoon.

The counselor at the abortion clinic swept through a bland description of the procedure—"a lot easier than pulling a tooth," Amanda heard her say—and an even more casual mention of the "products of conception" that would be gone when it was over. She knew that wasn't right and she started to cry. The counselor was reassuring: a lot of women felt emotional at a time like this. Would she like to think it over and come back?

As Daniel began to recap the dismal alternatives, Amanda cut him off and signed the consent, which neither of them read.

The doctor was pleasant, brisk, and behind schedule. Amanda didn't say much except for a half-question about how much it would hurt. He said "not much" as the stinging and the cramps broiled to a startling crescendo, but even they barely distracted her from the sounds of the suction and that weird thumping of tissue careening through the plastic tube. When it was all over she started crying again, but now from depths that were beyond the reach of the clinic staff (who had too many others to contend with during spring break), and way beyond Daniel's limited experience with love and loss.

The ride home was even quieter than the drive to the clinic. Daniel was attentive for the rest of the week but eventually began to grow weary of Amanda's moodiness, and especially her lack of physical affection. After a few weeks he suggested, in the gentlest language he could muster, that they take a time out from each other. She offered no resistance, and when the time out had extended beyond high school graduation, she stopped thinking about Daniel, "Together Forever," and the day at the clinic.

Amanda did go to college and dated a fair amount (more than she would have imagined in high school) but always kept her emotional distance—even during sex, which she found only vaguely enjoyable. Two years after college graduation Amanda met Seth, who dismantled her recent self-imposed moratorium on men. He asked disarming questions, kept her off balance, and resurrected emotions that had floated away with Daniel. After a fairy-tale courtship, a two-carat ring appeared one candlelit night, and the wedding followed six months later.

Seth had been one of the few men in her life who had expressed any interest in children, and after their second anniversary he began to make more frequent comments about having a family. During another of his irresistibly romantic dinners, he proposed a ceremonial burial of her birth control pills and, with a little help from a bottle of chardonnay, she accepted. But the next day she felt panic welling up, and in its wake depression rolled in like a fog. She manufactured reasons to avoid sex, especially halfway through her cycle, and began to awaken at odd hours, heart pounding like a trip-hammer, with memories of dreams—awful, surrealistic ones involving limbs and blood and crying babies.

When Seth's sister flew in with a new baby in tow, Amanda could barely carry on a conversation. Finally Seth became exasperated with her relentless funk and her unpredictable crying jags, and convinced her to talk about them. She had never said anything about her abortion—indeed, it had been shoved so far into the background of her mind that there was a momentary struggle to conjure up some of the details. As she gradually spilled out the story, he was calm, understanding, and vastly more consoling than even he could have imagined. He knew Amanda had not been a virgin on their wedding night, and she knew the same was true of him. He had not expected their prior experiences to intrude upon their own intimacy—what was past was past—but this abortion was another story, and it was wrecking their marriage. They needed help as soon as possible.

During their first visit with a marriage counselor, Amanda was encouraged to talk about the abortion. It was, after all, the problem that had prompted them to seek help. The counselor and Seth were both impressed, and Amanda surprised, by her unexpected tirade against Daniel, her parents' divorce, and even the abortionist whose name she had never heard. The experience proved to be a catharsis, and she felt much better for a day or two. But by the following week her depression was in full swing once again. During the next two visits, Amanda tried to revisit the abortion, but the counselor calmly recommended that she focus on current relationships. The abortion could not be the primary source of the anxious depression she was experiencing, she explained, and it was important not to dwell on it.

After three more sessions and a prescription from a psychiatrist, Amanda was more numb than agitated, profoundly discouraged, and thoroughly convinced that she had made as grand a mess of her life as anyone on the planet. She lay next to Seth for yet another interminable night, a thin layer of sweat across her forehead, drifting in and out of sleep, but mostly out. *How did I become so defective? Seth doesn't deserve all of this garbage.*

What's the point of all this counseling? It's costing so much, and we're not getting anywhere. And these lousy pills—I oughta flush them down the john, where the rest of my life is going. By the time Amanda walked into my office six months later, her marriage was in shambles and her self-concept was at an all-time low.

Stories similar to Amanda's have become familiar to me since my first conversation with a woman who was desperately seeking healing from the shame and grief of a past abortion. My heart is tender toward post-abortion women because I understand from my own past unfortunate choices how debilitating unresolved shame can become. It has been my great privilege and personal joy in recent years to help many women find peace and forgiveness after an abortion. My hope is that this book will help others discover healing from abortion's silent, solitary sorrow.

Part One

The Silent Epidemic

❖ ❖ ❖ ❖ ❖ ❖

Healing from the emotional pain of an
abortion *is* possible. Before we look at
how healing comes, we will lay the foundation of the causes, symptoms, and results of post-abortion pain.

Chapter One

The Experience No One Talks About

❖ ❖ ❖ ❖ ❖ ❖

Susan was visibly shaking as she sat in my office, midway through a therapy session. "I can't believe I just told you that. I have *never* told anyone about my abortion. It was seventeen years ago, and I swore I'd take that secret to my grave. I cannot believe I just told you!"

"Susan, I want to tell you, again, what I said when we started. Nothing leaves this room after we walk out. I want you to know that I will never share your personal information with anyone."

"It's more than that. It's . . . fear of what you must think about me now, I guess. I know you're a professional and would never tell anyone. But I can't stand it that another person now knows. And after I leave here, I won't be able to stop worrying about what you think of me now."

"Okay, so I'll tell you now, what I think of you, so you don't have to worry after you leave."

Susan looked at me doubtfully. "Okay."

"Susan, every person carries around some dreadful secret that, when they think about it, makes their cheeks flush with shame. And for most of us, that shameful secret is something connected to sex. So the truth is that I don't think any less of you because you told me about your abortion. In fact, I am really humbled and grateful that you trust me enough at this point to tell me something you've never told anyone else. Instead of distancing me from you, it has only made me feel much closer to you."

❖ ❖ ❖ ❖ ❖ ❖

Susan is one of many women I've talked to who are afraid to tell anyone of a past abortion. Even in a safe, nonjudgmental environment, it is difficult to share one's deepest secrets. I remember how I struggled to relinquish the darker episodes of my life to another person for the first time. I feared that my counselor would lose her understanding and think of me as defective and beyond redemption. In the same way, many women are desperately afraid of revealing the secret of their abortions.

Forty-three percent of all American women will choose to have an abortion at some point during their lifetime but hardly any of them talk about it. More than 35 million abortions have occurred in the United States since 1973. One out of every four babies conceived in America today will be aborted. More than 40 percent of women who will terminate their pregnancy this week have had at least one previous abortion. More than 18,000 of the abortions performed this year in the United States will be carried out after the fifth month of gestation. More than a million

American women will have an abortion this year.[1]
But hardly any of them talk about it.

Women share the most intimate details of
their lives with each other during a casual lunch,
but they choose not to talk about what they experienced during and after the most common medical procedure in America. An article in *U.S. News
and World Report* pondered the implications of the
statistic that 43 percent of American women have
had an abortion:

> That would mean that, for better or worse,
> abortion is as common a life experience for
> women as divorce and more than three times
> more common than breast cancer. It would
> mean that more than twice as many women
> have abortions as get college degrees. . . .
>
> The real reason the figure seems so im-
> plausible is that while women are willing to
> discuss the issue of abortion, they rarely talk
> about *their* abortions. . . . In America, abor-
> tion is discussed; abortions are not.[2]

Why is that? Abortion has been vigorously debated in our country for well over three decades.
We talk about it every election year, we hear it
discussed on talk shows, we see it whenever one
group or another, pro-life or pro-choice, carries
its signs and banners through the streets of Washington, D.C., or down Main Street, U.S.A. But for
all of this very public discussion, the typical experience of a woman who chooses to have an abortion is characterized not only by urgency—the

crisis needs to be resolved as soon as possible—but by secrecy. Few (if any) friends know about her decision, and even fewer are comfortable hearing about her feelings afterward. As a result, most women who have an abortion next week will walk through this important episode of their lives feeling very much alone, uncomfortable, and probably uncomforted as well.

My first experience counseling a woman for abortion-related emotional problems occurred in 1985. At that time I helped organize a crisis pregnancy center in our community, but I was not specifically seeking to counsel women who had post-abortion distress. Indeed, I wasn't even aware of it. But within a very short time, and unknown to one another, four women approached me asking to talk about their abortion experiences. Each one was open to the idea of forming a support group, and we met for about twelve weeks. I was genuinely astonished by what I learned from these brave women.

During the course of that first support group, I was impressed by the degree to which the abortion had been a solitary experience. For each person in the group, secrecy had been the hallmark of the entire process. The abortion decision had been made with little or no input from close friends or family. Each woman had either experienced the procedure on her own or perhaps had been accompanied by one other person who had long ago drifted out of her life. If any friends or relatives *did* know about the abortion, most were not comfortable allowing her to talk much about it afterward. These women carried their secrets like a heavy chain around the heart. Each believed that she was probably the only person in her sphere of relationships who had had an abortion. As a result, they felt not only defective but also extremely reluctant to broach this subject for fear of being judged.

The fact that these four women simultaneously crossed my path and were willing to share their solitary sorrow with me and with one another at first struck me as a fascinating coincidence. In retrospect, I see our meeting as truly providential. All of our lives were affected, but I believe mine most of all. Since then I have counseled with hundreds of women, both individually and in groups, who have felt a need to work through the emotional aftermath of an abortion. I have learned a great deal from them and have in turn helped train both professionals and lay counselors to walk post-abortion women through the process of healing.

As I worked through that first, all-important group, my curiosity led me to look for books and professional literature that might offer some perspective on this problem. What I found was a surprising scarcity of research. I also found—and this was *not* surprising—a passionate debate already in progress between those who felt that abortion nearly always brought emotional relief and those whose experiences with post-abortion women suggested otherwise. (A summary of this debate may be found in appendix 1, "A Brief History of Post-Abortion Syndrome.")

I have counseled with these women since 1985. Nearly twenty years of sporadic and contradictory research hasn't dulled any of their pain, nor has the longstanding debate over the existence of their distress offered them comfort. They merely want relief from the guilt and grief they feel long after aborting their child.

This book is written for them, and for those who are striving to offer them compassionate help.

Who Experiences Post-Abortion Syndrome?

Author Frederica Mathewes-Green wrote the following words in a pro-life magazine article a number of years ago,

> No one wants an abortion as she wants an ice cream cone or a Porsche. She wants an abortion as an animal, caught in a trap, wants to gnaw off its own leg.[3]

Mathewes-Green was surprised to find her analogy quoted some time later in pro-choice materials as well. It was in fact "Quote of the Week" in Planned Parenthood's *Public Affairs Action Letter*, and "Quote of the Month" in the *Pro-Choice Network Newsletter*. In response, she observed, "Apparently pro-choice partisans could agree with pro-lifers that, no matter what their political differences, abortion was a miserable choice."[4]

Regardless of one's position in the intense,

ongoing debate about abortion in our country, very few people—especially those who have had an abortion themselves—would ever consider this procedure, or the decision to have one, to be a casual event. Powerful instincts, profound moral sentiments, and strong emotions (especially fear) are always stirred by a crisis pregnancy, and abortion does not permanently banish them. The intensity of this experience and the secrecy that surrounds it frequently set the stage for problems in the future, both immediate and distant. A number of counselors and psychologists who have explored this issue have identified a condition they call post-abortion syndrome (or PAS). PAS is defined as an ongoing inability to:

◆ Process the painful thoughts and emotions—especially guilt, anger, and grief—that arise from one or more crisis pregnancies and subsequent abortions.
◆ Identify (and grieve) the loss that has been experienced.
◆ Come to peace with God, oneself, and others involved in the pregnancy and abortion decision.

PAS involves a variety of symptoms—psychological, physical, and spiritual—that will be reviewed in detail in the next chapter. It should be made clear from the outset, however, that having an abortion does not universally bring about long-term distress. There are a number of risk factors that have been identified in research studies, and borne out by my personal observations with hundreds of post-abortion women, that predispose a woman undergoing an abortion to emotional problems later in life. Of these the most important are *coercion* and *ambivalence*.

Coercion

Given the importance of the word choice among those who champion abortion rights, it is a sobering reality that many women who enter abortion clinics on any given day are caving in to other people in their lives. Some typical scenarios:

◆ A boyfriend who has declared, in no uncertain terms, that "it's the baby or me." In the most blatant situations, he views his pregnant lover literally as a broken toy that needs to be repaired, or else he will move on to another playground.

◆ A husband who is convinced that "this isn't the right time" (financially, career-wise, etc.) to have the first baby or another child.

◆ Parents who are sure that they are acting in their daughter's best interests and protecting her future by terminating her pregnancy.

◆ Less commonly, a sibling—especially one who is worried about the impact of a crisis pregnancy on the family—or a friend who feels he or she is looking out for the pregnant woman's best interests by pushing for an abortion.

Coercion can at times be shockingly physical. I

have personally been involved in cases where parents have kept a teenage daughter literally under lock and key, blocked communication with anyone who might have a differing opinion, and then spirited her off to a clinic at which an abortion was carried out—sometimes while she is restrained. More often other forms of pressure are applied. The baby's biological father may put the relationship on the line ("We're through if you don't have an abortion.") or the woman's basic needs may be threatened ("If you want to have that baby, you'll have to move out!").

Tracy came to one of my first post-abortion groups and was clearly agitated over what had happened to her a few years before. She was married to an ambitious and dominating man who had been convinced that the size of their family should precisely match the size of their home. In his view, each child must have his or her own bedroom. When Tracy became pregnant with their third child, she was delighted—but he was adamant that their home wasn't big enough for another family member. He therefore scheduled an abortion at a local clinic and instructed her to keep the appointment. However, when the time came to sign the consent, Tracy was so distraught that she left the clinic.

When her husband learned that she had failed to carry out her assignment, he was furious. He scheduled another appointment and took her to the clinic himself, complaining repeatedly about the amount of time he was wasting when he had other important work to do. He stood over her while she tearfully signed the consent, and the abortion was carried out. Months later, he could not understand why she was so withdrawn and why she was so uninterested in having sex.

As Tracy completed the support group and some individual counseling, she made significant progress working through the pain connected with the abortion. Unfortunately, her husband would not concede that he had coerced her into having the abortion. Their marriage deteriorated, and they separated a year later.

Ambivalence

While coercion occurs in a limited numbers of cases, ambivalence is very common. In one sense, it is rare that a woman who undergoes an abortion is *not* ambivalent. It is important for a woman with an unexpected pregnancy to sort through her immediate circumstances in order to recognize her core emotions: What would she feel about this pregnancy, about having this child, if her circumstances were more favorable? Very few say that they would have had the abortion if everything had been ideal: supportive mate or family, adequate financial and personal resources, excellent physical and emotional health, and so forth.

Pro-choice activists frequently claim that "religious dogma" and outmoded sexual taboos are the primary source of personal and cultural resistance to abortion. But when a woman has just learned she is pregnant, deeper instincts that transcend both her moral code and her circumstances quickly begin to stir. The knowledge that a new human being is growing inside of her sets off an unmistakable inner spark. Whether she acknowledges it or not, her universe is a different place from that point on.

In the Crisis Pregnancy Center setting, while waiting for the results of a pregnancy test, I have talked to women who say in no uncertain terms that they will have an abortion if the test is positive. But if the test is negative, I have often seen a brief flicker of disappointment. The possibility of creating a new life comes wrapped in a profound sense of awe and wonder. Call it what you will—maternal instinct or the divine order of creation—it is a unique and powerful gift to women in every culture, and no cultural drift or political ideology can drive it out.

Women facing an abortion decision also feel ambivalent if they know basic facts about human development and some details of abortion procedures. Crisis Pregnancy Centers have been forthright in providing information about fetal development, and many facilities reinforce it with ultrasound images of the woman's own baby. As women become more aware of the humanity of the developing baby, they become more ambivalent about abortion.

Abortion clinics seek to minimize this ambivalence by using misleading euphemisms for the human fetus ("uterine contents," "pregnancy tissue," "products of conception," and others). This terminology has led millions of women to believe that an abortion merely removes a shapeless wad of unwanted protoplasm, much like draining an abscess or taking out a diseased appendix. Sooner or later, however, most find out that this was not the case. Perhaps the realization comes during a prenatal ultrasound or childbirth class during a later pregnancy, or while watching a program such as the PBS/Nova documentary *The Miracle of Life.* When the lights go on, feelings of betrayal and resentment soon follow: *I had an abortion at ten weeks, and what they sucked out of me looked like THAT? Why didn't they tell me that what I was about to abort was a baby and not a blob of tissue?*

Today more women entering an abortion clinic know who is being aborted and what the procedure will do to him or her. Without the temporary balm of denial, regrets and emotional struggles may arise much sooner after the abortion. Needless to say, any of these emotional aftershocks are likely to be intensified if the woman has other grounds for mixed emotions. *(I really would have liked to have the baby, if only. . . .)* Later on, when the reason for having the abortion has faded into memory and seems less compelling, the loss of the child may move to the emotional foreground. This is especially true, and particularly poignant, if she is not able to conceive later in life.

Cassie became pregnant during her senior year of college. There was no confusion about her moral stance regarding abortion. The first time she had considered the abortion issue in junior high she decided it was an immoral choice. But as the eldest child of parents who had never graduated college, she felt tremendous pressure to graduate on schedule. So she had an abortion in early March. She went through a flurry of graduation celebrations in a painful haze of conflicting emotions, bouncing between satisfaction in her parents' pride and dismay at her choice to abort her baby.

I first met with Cassie when she was twenty-eight. She had been married for five years and seemed to be infertile. The glow of graduation had long passed, but she had trouble forgetting the secret of her abortion.

Other Risk Factors

In addition to coercion and ambivalence, a number of other circumstances may increase the likelihood and severity of emotional distress after abortion, both in the immediate and distant future.

Religious upbringing and spiritual convictions. Many women have abortions while believing that God specifically disapproves, thus violating religious teachings and principles taught for years at home or in church. The toughest clients at a pregnancy center often come from families that are prominent in a local church (including those of elders and pastors). These women often head to abortion clinics out of a need to conceal sexual misconduct, a fear of disappointing parents who are highly esteemed in the church, and an unwillingness to bring public reproach to the family (or even cause the loss of a father's pastorate). Yet they will most likely regret this decision later in life.

I have spoken with dozens of young women from religious families who came to our crisis center for a pregnancy test, and I have heard many variations of the following statement: "I already understand this is a baby and I do believe that abortion is murder. But you don't understand . . . my parents don't even think I'm having sex! I will *not* make them pay for my mistake. I know that I'll never be okay with this, but I'd rather face God's wrath than disappoint my parents."

One or more previous abortions. In post-abortion support groups, women who have had more than one abortion usually admit to feeling intensely defective. *Anyone might make this mistake once. How could I have gone back and repeated the same destructive choices over and over?* Sadly, about 40 percent of post-abortion women in the United States have had more than one abortion. In the past five years, I have heard from more and more women who have had two or more abortions.

Second and third trimester abortions. Not only are these procedures more complicated (and far more gruesome to those who have not been physically sedated), but they are also more likely to confront the woman with the harsh reality that her "product of conception" was clearly a human being. Furthermore, procedures carried out later in pregnancy often result from delays in decisions due to personal conflict or indecision.

The first woman I ever dealt with who had

experienced a second trimester abortion waited months for her boyfriend to make good on his promise to marry her and give her the "happily ever after" ending. When she was in her sixth month of pregnancy, Prince Charming made a hasty exit from her fairy tale and rode off with a thinner heroine. Distraught, she went through a saline abortion and was severely traumatized when she delivered a dead baby after four hours of intense labor.

Abortions for fetal abnormalities or other medical problems. One would think that these abortions would represent the most justifiable, conflict-free decisions. But they may generate emotional strain later on, for a number of reasons. First, the defect may not have been diagnosed until a later stage of pregnancy—for example, following an amniocentesis in the second trimester. This in turn requires a more traumatic procedure if abortion is chosen. Second, there is often strong outside pressure to abort a fetus known or suspected to be defective, even if that possibility is very small. Husband, family members, and especially the physician (who traditionally has been cast in the role of The One Responsible for Delivering a Flawless Infant) may all join a chorus pleading for her to spare them the disappointment and extra work involved in rearing a handicapped child. All of these voices will also tend to push for a decision *as soon as possible*, adding to the feeling later on that the decision was railroaded. Third, a woman may abort a child with a defect—for example, Down syndrome— that she later feels she could have lived with, perhaps after learning about a network of support groups and resources for families with children having that particular problem. Some may think, *I aborted my own child because I didn't have the compassion or the guts to play the cards that I was dealt.*

I'll never forget the first woman I talked to who had aborted her Down syndrome fetus at the strong urging of her physician and family. When she later came into contact with a family who was happily rearing a Down syndrome child *whom they had specifically requested to adopt,* she felt betrayed by the doctor and angry because she had allowed herself to be talked into a fast decision before she could do any research.

A variation on this issue involves the *potential* defect. This occurs when a woman learns that she has become pregnant while taking a particular medication, or after contracting an illness (such as chickenpox) during her pregnancy. She is given dire warnings by her physician about the terrible damage that this might cause to the baby, but often without a clear sense of the actual odds of a bad outcome. If she has an abortion and later discovers that the likelihood of a problem was actually quite small, the emotional fallout later in life will be greater.

A dear friend and I had the joy of delivering our first children two days apart. A few years later, she developed chickenpox two months into a second pregnancy. Her obstetrician gave her severe warnings about the risk of delivering a deformed infant and strongly urged her to have an abortion. She was morally opposed to abortion, however, and declined to take this step. With some additional research, she was relieved to learn that the risk of her baby's having a congenital defect was only about 2 percent—far less than the odds she had been given by her doctor. She delivered a perfectly healthy son seven months later.

Abortion of a pregnancy resulting from rape. At face value, this situation would appear to offer an unambiguous justification for an abortion. Yet some of the same factors that complicate an abortion for a fetal defect can also create emotional difficulty following abortion for rape. Pressure from others to abort, and a sense of urgency to do so, frequently come into play and may lead the woman to question her decision later in life. Even more compelling may be the dawning of a conviction (usually after a number of years have passed) that the evil, criminal act of rape was not the baby's fault, and that half of the baby's genetic material came from her.

I have been genuinely surprised on several occasions to hear a rape victim express resentment over the rejection of her baby by those who recommended abortion. "They kept saying that this was the rapist's baby," she tells me, "and that it was evil. But it was my baby, too. I really felt like I was raped twice—first when sex was forced on me, and again when the abortion was forced on me."

Being awake during the procedure. Most abortions are performed during the first three months of pregnancy using local anesthesia. As a result, millions of women have had wide-awake, often jolting abortion experiences. The dilating of the cervix (intensely painful if the anesthetic isn't adequate), the whirring of the vacuum, the suctioning, the thumping of fetal tissue passing through the tube—remembered vividly by many as "the sound of pieces of my baby being sucked away"—all leave vivid, indelible memories. A woman who has experienced an abortion later in pregnancy may have to grapple with even more disturbing mental images; for example, a scalded (and occasionally still living) premature infant delivered a few hours after the injection of concentrated saline into the uterus.

A recent pregnancy with a "wanted" child. A few years earlier, during a crisis pregnancy, a woman may have heard the term "products of conception" at the abortion clinic. Now, she uses her own phrase—"my baby," the object of great care and concern—during the first or second prenatal check at the obstetrician's office. In each situation, the stage of her pregnancy is the same. At some point before her due date, she may leaf through a book that contains exquisite photographs of life before birth in order to see what her baby looks like. As she scans the pictures of the eight- or ten- or twelve-week fetus, there is a pause, a silent gasp. *This looks like a baby, but it's just ten weeks into the pregnancy—the same point at* *which I had the abortion. There really isn't any difference between the one now growing inside me and the one that was killed during my abortion.*

A variation on this conflict occurs when a woman has an abortion after one or more children have been born. In this case, it is likely that her previous pregnancy has given her some idea what the aborted baby might look like, and this could intensify her ambivalence about the impending procedure. In addition, she must eventually acknowledge that, in a very real sense, aborting one child calls into question the value of the others. "I could have had *you* aborted!" (Or, worse, "I *should* have had you aborted!") might be the most destructive verbal grenade an exasperated mother could lob on an unruly child in the heat of battle. But while few women would actually utter such a toxic sentiment to one of their children, many have been unsettled by the thought that a particular collection of circumstances—timing, relationships, resources, even the availability of abortion—could have snuffed out the life of a son or daughter now standing before them.

Inability to conceive after one or more abortions. Few situations are more poignant than the plight of a woman grappling with infertility after aborting one or more pregnancies earlier in life. "I aborted the only child I ever conceived" are the words of some of the most profoundly sorrowful women on the planet.

Past or current turbulence, emotional and oth-

erwise. Without a doubt, a woman's emotional stability will shape her response to a crisis pregnancy, an abortion, and the fallout from terminating her pregnancy. Indeed, pro-choice advocates and abortion providers who discount the extent and severity of post-abortion distress invariably attribute *any* such difficulty to a woman's personal emotional weather. Focusing (or obsessing) on one or more previous abortions is said to be nothing more than a manifestation of her underlying anxiety and depression. Treat that, they argue, and the abortion will become a nonissue.

In reality, the same factors that contribute to anxiety and depression—past emotional trauma, abuse, major losses early in life, genetic and biochemical factors, and current life stresses—also increase the risk for post-abortion distress. And there are some women for whom the issues surrounding abortion are just the tip of an immense iceberg. But years of conversations with post-abortion women have made it abundantly clear to me that abortion isn't merely a handy scapegoat for women who don't want to come to grips with other issues. Later in this chapter I will describe how life stresses, both past and present, can play a significant role in the development of post-abortion distress, whether or not a woman has struggled with anxiety and depression before.

Abortion when very young and unmarried. Several of the risk factors just mentioned commonly converge on the adolescent abortion: coercion, ambivalence (about much of life), emotional turmoil, procedures later in pregnancy (because fear and denial may stall her decision-making process), sexual abuse/rape, and even one or more previous pregnancies and abortions. We will look at post-abortion issues arising from teenage pregnancies in appendix 3.

A change of heart. Many women who join post-abortion support groups have had a recent spiritual awakening or renewal. Usually this has reoriented (or completely reversed) their values regarding human life or has raised issues of accountability to God for events in the past, including one or more abortions. Choices that seemed compelling, reasonable, and right in a previous crisis may now be viewed as terrible mistakes or outright transgressions for which repentance is necessary. Others who change their mind do so strictly on secular grounds, usually because of a confrontation with the facts of prenatal development or abortion techniques.

Many whose lives take a new course become champions of the pro-life cause. Others feel the need to "labor in the trenches" at Crisis Pregnancy Centers or other ministries as a form of penance. (Some even carry a notion that they are obliged to work a certain number of years—usually five to seven—for each abortion they have had.) A few deal with more severe issues of guilt, or expectations that God will send them a calamity, such as the death of one of their children or a deformed baby, as punishment for their prior misdeeds. Needless to say, the spiritual dimen-

41

sions of the post-abortion experience are highly significant, and we will look at their role in the healing process in some detail in chapter 5.

Who does not experience PAS? The fact that there are so many risk factors for post-abortion syndrome raises a provocative question: Are there situations in which the likelihood of emotional consequences from an abortion would be minimal? Turning all of the risk factors inside out, one could speculate about what the ultimate "no regrets" abortion might look like:

◆ The woman is well past adolescence.
◆ She comes from a family in which abortion is not only an acceptable choice for an un-planned pregnancy but also has been experienced by several trusted female relatives who talk about it openly.
◆ There is no significant past trauma or history of loss.
◆ Her decision is well thought out and not co-erced, and all feelings have been explored ahead of time with a seasoned counselor.
◆ Her concept of her pregnancy is that it involves a minuscule amount of tissue that has no intrinsic worth or humanity and no soul residing within it (so that she won't meet the baby "on the other side" after she dies).
◆ She has excellent rapport with the doctor, who knows her quite well and feels that this is the best decision for her.
◆ The abortion procedure is done slowly and

carefully, perhaps under anesthesia, and there are no physical complications.

◆ She has a lot of support for her decision, both before and after the procedure, and she has a viable arena in which to talk about her feelings afterwards.

Needless to say, this highly idealized scenario is hardly the norm, but rather a fantasy. It bears little resemblance to the tough realities of the vast majority of crisis pregnancies and the chilly mechanics of the typical abortion experience.

How Does Post-Abortion Syndrome Develop?

Those who have counseled post-abortion women have identified a number of recurring themes and common pathways that lead to the development of PAS. Of course, each woman's story has its own unique flavor, cast of characters, and order of events. But all stories are affected by the many risk factors just described and most include the following sequence of elements:

1. The pregnancy is a crisis. First, the pregnancy has potential consequences, which appear disastrous, both in the immediate and distant future. It involves bad timing, the wrong relationship, adverse circumstances, a sexual misadventure or coerced sex, lack of resources, endangered plans, a medical problem for mother and/or baby, or (more likely) a combination of several of these.

There is a great deal of fear and anxiety, and with it a driving need for an immediate and often secret solution.

2. A moral dilemma develops. The woman then becomes aware that terminating her pregnancy will violate her own moral code, whether or not she has taken a definite position against abortion. As I have noted already, the instinct to protect and nurture the child growing within is "hardwired," in my opinion, transcending time and culture. Bonding with one's offspring is not the result of social convention or formal teaching. Its impact may be clouded, or even drowned out, by the clamor of circumstances. But this inner voice may also be powerfully enhanced if a woman holds conscious beliefs about the value of human life and especially if she identifies the entity growing inside her as a human being—more specifically, her son or daughter—rather than a wad of unwanted tissue. Even if there is no apparent inner conflict at the time of an abortion, events later in life frequently bring these moral issues to the emotional foreground.

3. The expedient solution—an abortion—brings transient relief. For better or worse, the abortion means the crisis has been dealt with. This phase typically lasts for a few days or weeks. In recent years, however, it appears to be shortening, probably because more women are being exposed to the basic facts of fetal development via ultrasonography and programs on educational television.

4. The moral dilemma eventually resurfaces. Along with the moral dilemma comes painful memories and emotions. For a period of several days or even weeks the abortion decision is now called into question. *Did I really do the right thing?*

5. The pain, if not acknowledged and dealt with, is suppressed using a variety of coping strategies and avoidance behaviors. Even in a culture where sharing one's feelings and seeking counseling are socially acceptable, several factors tend to block openness when the issue is an abortion. Few people anticipate that the post-abortion woman might need to grieve the loss of her pregnancy. After all, the abortion was presumably her choice, and those who supported her decision (along with the clinic staff and the culture at large) have made the assumption that "relief" from a crisis pregnancy is spelled a-b-o-r-t-i-o-n. In a real sense, she is denied permission to admit that this was not in fact the case. Further, she had not anticipated a difficult experience and is surprised by her emotional response. She is not aware that others have had similar responses following an abortion and the secretive nature of the abortion experience discourages ventilating to others about it. The emotional, psychological, and even physical responses to this pain are frightening, highly unpleasant, and confusing. In order to keep the feelings at bay, a variety of defense mechanisms may be marshaled:

❖ **Denial**: a refusal to accept the reality of

the problem (*I don't really feel anything* or *This can't be about the abortion*), or disowning the conflict altogether (*I didn't do anything wrong*).

◇ **Rationalization**: a rehearsing of all of the reasons why the abortion seemed to be justified. (*There were no other options. My boyfriend/husband wouldn't stay with me if I had the baby. I'm a full-time student. I couldn't support myself, let alone a baby. Even if I had the baby, I couldn't stand to give her away to someone else.*)

◇ **Repression**: memories of the experience (and its accompanying emotions) are pushed into the background. In extreme cases, a woman later in life may be unable to remember that she even *had* one or more abortions.

◇ **Avoidance**: staying away from situations or information that might bring the conflict back into the foreground. If she has seen a lot of babies in the supermarket during the afternoon, she starts shopping at midnight. If the church is having a special program for Sanctity of Life Sunday, this becomes the ideal weekend to sleep in.

◇ **Compensation**: an ongoing effort through good works—serving in church ministries, being a "Supermom," even actively participating in the pro-life movement—to pay the moral debt incurred by the abortion.

◇ **Reaction formation**: the unpleasant feelings are not only pushed away, but the exact opposite of those feelings are vigorously professed—often while fighting back tears. *(I have never, ever regretted having the abortion. It was the best thing I could have done, and since that time I have had the best years of my life.)*

6. These efforts to push away her pain may continue more or less successfully for years. They prevent a woman from working through the grieving process normally associated with a pregnancy loss. Such strategies also require a significant amount of energy to maintain. As a result, after many months or years, a series of major events—for example, marriage, one or more "wanted" pregnancies, the twenty-four-hour responsibility of rearing small children, a spiritual conversion, or any number of ongoing life issues—can wear down and eventually overwhelm these coping mechanisms.

At this point one or more symptoms of post-abortion syndrome begin to emerge.

Chapter Two

No Longer Coping

❖ ❖ ❖ ❖ ❖ ❖

Jeanne entwined her fingers in the small cro-
cheted pillow that sits on the couch in my office.
"I can't get away from it. It's like being caught in a
Twilight Zone episode, except that the end of the
show never comes. There's no way out of this. I
don't even know why I made this appointment.
There's nothing you can say to make this go away
or make me feel better. It seemed like the perfect
solution at the time, you know? And I was fine with
it for a long time. But now it haunts me as I try to
drift off to sleep. I wake up in the middle of the night
and I can't turn my brain off. The phrase keeps
repeating over and over: 'I killed my own child.' I'm
going to go crazy if I can't turn this voice off."

❖ ❖ ❖ ❖ ❖ ❖

My heart went out to Jeanne. I remembered my
own first session in a counselor's office. The same
feelings of "I'm losing control of my life" threatened to overwhelm me as I said them out loud
for the first time. By the time a woman reaches
out for help for consuming pain from an abortion, she will express desperate concerns:

"I don't know what is going on with me."
"I feel as if I'm losing control of everything."
"I walk into a room and forget why I'm there."
"I can't control the sudden crying."
"I feel as though I'm losing my mind—is this the beginning of insanity?"

Like a toxic spill that can no longer be kept out of the local water supply, painful symptoms are now contaminating the flow of her daily life. None of this develops overnight, however. In the previous chapter, I described a process in which a woman suppresses the conflict surrounding her abortion experience but eventually reaches a point at which her coping strategies no longer are effective. When this occurs, she will experience one or more—usually several—of the following symptoms:

◆ Guilt
◆ Anxiety
◆ Psychological "numbing"
◆ Depression
◆ Re-experiencing events related to the abortion
◆ Fertility, pregnancy, and bonding issues
◆ Survivor guilt
◆ Self-abusive/self-destructive behaviors
◆ Anniversary reactions
◆ Brief psychotic disorder

Guilt

When a woman asks for help dealing with the

aftermath of one or more abortions, the first thing she usually says is that her sense of guilt has become overwhelming, a crushing burden she can no longer carry. The guilt she feels extends beyond mere shame that her deeds were discovered, or a vague sense that she has violated some rules laid down at home, church, or school. This is definitely not "false guilt," a discomfort generated over something that she isn't really convinced is wrong. It is an aching, abiding conviction that she has broken her own moral code—the set of values that she has accepted and internalized as determining what is right and wrong. These may certainly encompass what she has heard over the years (especially from her parents), but their defining characteristic is that, whatever their source, she truly buys into them.

Guilt related to abortion often becomes particularly intense because:

◆ Abortion entails the deliberate taking of an innocent human life. The more convinced a woman becomes that this was indeed a human being, and not worthless tissue, the more acute her discomfort. Often that conviction arrives years after the event, but it is now not uncommon for women to proceed with an abortion even with a clear understanding that a baby is being aborted. When that is the case, guilt may come sooner, rather than later.

◆ Abortion doesn't merely take an innocent life at random. It takes the life of the woman's own child. Her decision thus overrides a powerful instinct to defend her own baby. This primal urge is not easily squelched and often remains vocal later in life when the circumstances surrounding the abortion may seem far less compelling.

◆ For those who take to heart the teachings of the Old and New Testaments, abortion often has far more profound implications. The deliberate terminating of the life of one's son or daughter doesn't merely fly in the face of the laws of nature, but it also violates (to paraphrase Thomas Jefferson) the laws of nature's God. If a primary tenet of a woman's moral code is that she is to "love the Lord her God with all her heart, mind, soul, and strength," and the Lord her God abhors the shedding of innocent blood, then her participation in such an act will be a heavy burden to bear.

Women (and others involved in the abortion decision) may use a variety of defense mechanisms, especially denial and rationalization, to keep guilt at bay. Counseling offered by abortion providers or their ideological supporters may attempt to bolster a woman's defenses against guilt: "The abortion really was in your best interest. . . ." But when those personal defenses begin to crumble for whatever reason, the impact of guilt can become overwhelming. When we've labored long and hard *not* to feel guilty, the flood proves to be intense and uncontrollable when the dam finally breaks.

Anxiety

Anxiety is another common emotion for post-abortion women. Anxiety is defined as "an unpleasant emotional and physical state of apprehension." Among post-abortion women, anxiety typically accompanies intense feelings of guilt, but it may also arise from avoidance behaviors. (See the next section.) Anxiety is experienced not only as the familiar symptoms of worry, poor concentration, and difficulty relaxing, but also as a variety of physical symptoms such as headache, dizziness, pounding heart, abdominal cramps, and muscle tightness, among others. It may coexist with depression, and both conditions may disrupt sleep. Difficulty falling asleep, nightmares, and/or frequent wakening throughout the night will all magnify the impact of other symptoms.

For some, these ongoing discomforts are punctuated by full-blown panic episodes that bring normal activities to a screeching halt. I have observed an increasing number of post-abortion women who have (or appear to be on the verge of developing) panic disorder. In fact, it is not unusual to start a post-abortion support group in which at least one woman is already using a substantial daily dose of medication to prevent or extinguish anxiety attacks. These episodes are extraordinarily uncomfortable, and if untreated can lead to a disabling fear of venturing any distance from one's home. Jane experienced this fear.

Jane called me several years ago after hearing that I was starting a support group for post-abortion issues. She had recently lost her job because of frequent absences that were caused by her fear of being seized by a panic attack whenever she left her apartment. Like many individuals with unpredictable panic episodes, she had withdrawn into a self-imposed imprisonment. She was taking eight to ten Xanax tablets per day in an effort to ward off the attacks, and she required a Herculean effort to drive to my office for the first session. After ten weeks in the support group, however, she had reduced her Xanax intake to one or two tablets per day and had succeeded in finding another job.

If a woman suffers from significant anxiety or a panic disorder, this does not automatically mean that she is dealing with post-abortion distress. Unfortunately, however, the emotional fallout from an abortion is frequently overlooked as a possible contributor to anxiety. If the issues arising from the abortion are not addressed, her recovery may be impeded.

Avoidance Behaviors

Another symptom of post-abortion syndrome is avoidance. Under normal circumstances, we instinctively avoid situations that we have experienced as unpleasant. The post-abortion woman is no exception. She will often avoid anything that reminds her of pregnancy and children. For example, she may refuse baby shower invitations or change channels during a diaper commercial.

Occasionally avoidance behaviors evolve into outright phobias, which may interfere with normal activities. For example, a visit to a doctor's office may set off such intense apprehension that routine exams may be delayed for years or avoided altogether. On a regular basis I deal with post-abortion women who haven't had a pap smear for the better part of a decade because of the negative emotions associated with it.

Psychological "Numbing"

This symptom does not take years to surface but rather begins soon after the abortion. For some women it is the most profound consequence of abortion in terms of the extent of its impact and the amount of effort required to reverse it. Anyone who has experienced a highly painful loss may develop an instinct to guard against situations that might bring such intense pain again. This drive for self-protection is like a vow: "Nothing will *ever* hurt me that badly again!" The vow may be unconscious, but it is no less fervent or long-lasting—indeed, it usually demonstrates *more* permanence than most conscious vows. But this mindset comes at a terrible price: it hampers a woman's ability to enter fully into an intimate relationship with another human being.

Julius Fogel, M.D. has practiced in two medical specialties—obstetrics/gynecology and psychiatry. In the former role he performed more than 20,000 abortions. As a psychiatrist, he subsequently made an incisive observation:

> There is no question about the emotional grief and mourning following an abortion. It shows up in various forms. I've had patients who had abortions a year or two ago . . . but it still bothers them. . . . There is no question in my mind that we are disturbing a life process. . . . Often the trauma may sink into the unconscious and never surface during a woman's lifetime. . . . [But] a psychological price is paid. I can't say exactly what. It may be alienation, it may be a pushing away from human warmth, perhaps a hardening of the maternal instinct. Something happens on the deeper levels of a woman's consciousness when she destroys a pregnancy. I know that as a psychiatrist.[1]

This "pushing away from human warmth" is something I see repeatedly among post-abortion women, many of whom unconsciously keep their emotions on a "flat line" in an effort to avoid any vulnerability. But like the patient with a cardiac "flat line" in the emergency room, these women have lost an essential part of their humanity—in this case, the ability to connect and develop emotional intimacy with another human being.

Achieving emotional intimacy requires a prolonged process, a dance of sorts that takes years to perfect. (Needless to say, it is a far cry from physical intimacy, which can occur between people who have no connection whatsoever, or who even despise one another.) It involves a sequence of exchanges, occurring hundreds or even thousands of times, in which one person offers the other a little piece of personal information that isn't normally available for public consumption. For the process to continue in a healthy way, each person must prove trustworthy with an increasing knowledge of the other's weaknesses, mistakes, and shame. The message that comes back must be, "I understand clearly what you are telling me about yourself, and it only serves to endear you to me, not distance me from you." Ideally, the dance draws the individuals closer and closer, until each is fully known and accepted by the other.

This delicate process can be disrupted or derailed by any number of everyday glitches—miscommunication, time pressure, distractions, lack of common interests, differences in personality, and so forth. But it will be stopped cold, even when there is enough mutual attraction to jump-start a relationship, if one person is incapable of "emotionally undressing" in front of the other. This inability to move toward emotional intimacy will often be missed during a red-hot romance (which on the surface *seems* emotionally intimate, but in fact physical intimacy may mask the problem), or even during a prolonged engagement. But it will have a profound effect on a marriage, where one person tries (often for years) to move closer while the other is unconsciously pushing away. The turning point in my own marriage involved my finally being able to allow Paul to know the weakest parts of me and to find out that he loved me anyway. It is not uncommon for women seeking post-abortion counseling to be mired in profound communication problems and general dissatisfaction within their significant relationships. Indeed, I have found that marital discontentment is an issue in therapy with a majority of post-abortion clients.

Depression

Many women become clinically depressed after abortion. Most experience some of the following symptoms:

Sad mood. A woman seeking help because of a previous abortion almost always describes a prevailing negative mood. This can range from "feeling a little down" to profound sadness arising from painful memories flowing into her conscious mind.

Sudden and uncontrollable crying episodes. A generalized sense of sadness may be punctuated by more disruptive episodes of crying or feeling "out of control." This emotional incontinence may cause a woman to wonder if she is "going insane" and often prods her (or those around her) to seek help.[2]

Sense of worthlessness. Symptoms of depression typically include self-devaluation, ranging from a vague sense of inadequacy to feelings of utter worthlessness. When the post-abortion woman's carefully constructed defense mechanisms begin to crumble, and she confronts the stark reality of her decision to end her child's life, her guilt over this act can precipitate an acute plunge in self-esteem. Any abandonment or rejection she felt from the father of the baby, her parents, or her friends will accelerate this downward spiral. If she also feels alienated from God because of the abortion, she may literally feel like the scum of the earth.

Sleep and appetite disturbances. Both eating and sleeping problems are common in depression, and each may have a physical (biochemical) basis that responds to antidepressant medication. But these may also have psychological and spiritual origins. For example, hypersomnia (excessive sleeping) may represent a temporary escape from freshly surfaced emotional pain. On the other hand, unpleasant and intrusive thoughts may cause problems falling or staying asleep. Overeating may serve as a readily available method of finding temporary comfort. Or, emotional turbulence may cause appetite to dwindle.

Disruption of sexual drive. Sexual desire is usually reduced, if not absent, during a depression. For the post-abortion woman, sex often becomes the "enemy," not only for its association with the abortion but often for another important reason. Of the hundreds of post-abortion women I have counseled since 1985, at least half have reported being the victims of some kind of early childhood sexual abuse. Statistics from various studies indicate that between 50 and 75 percent of pregnant adolescents have a history of sexual abuse.[3] Early sexual abuse and other sexual assaults are likely to disrupt a woman's future experiences of intimacy, love, and sex. They also impair her judgment in making sexual decisions, and increase her vulnerability to further sexual victimization. Needless to say, assessing and dealing with sexual damage is part of the healing process for a majority of post-abortion woman.

Reduced motivation. Depression also causes everyday problems to seem colossal. This may reach a point at which getting out of bed in the morning (or afternoon) takes major effort. Tackling a major issue—especially the emotional fallout from an abortion—may feel like attempting to climb Mt. Everest in the dead of winter.

Loss of normal sources of pleasure. A depressed person often experiences *anhedonia:* the inability to find pleasure in things that formerly provided enjoyment. Trimming the roses, finishing that needlepoint, putting photos in the family album, sitting in the sunshine with a freshly brewed glass of iced tea—these everyday experiences that were once pleasant "vacations" from the demands of life now seem not only joyless but pointless.

Disruption in interpersonal relationships. The woman experiencing a growing depression feels like a black hole in space: everything is collapsing inward under a relentless, crushing force, and nothing is going outward. If she is disciplined and stoic, she may override this feeling enough to grind through the daily routines of life, but there will be no energy remaining for emotional intimacy with another person. She is convinced that her bleak center will not be understood, or that it should not be inflicted on anyone else. She may feel it is pointless to attempt to explain it, even to someone with whom she usually bares her soul. In time, her prediction that no one will be able to join her in this place of hopelessness becomes a self-fulfilling prophecy. Those who would normally reach out to her eventually tire of receiving nothing in return and give up trying.

Thoughts of suicide. When I am talking with a depressed client who has children at home, I often hear the reassurance, "No matter how rotten I might feel, I would never actually hurt myself, because I couldn't do that to my kids." The presence of another person "to live for" (especially a child) is a powerful restraint on the urge to end one's life. However, if a woman has aborted one or more children and feels that there is no one in her world who truly needs her, then an important barrier to self-destruction is absent.

A 1987 study of women who suffered from post-abortion syndrome found that 60 percent had experienced suicidal thoughts, 28 percent had attempted suicide, and 18 percent had attempted suicide more than once.[4] A 1996 Finnish study of women who committed suicide within one year of a pregnancy found that the suicide rate associated with induced abortion was 34.7 per 100,000 women, compared to 18.1 for women following miscarriage and 5.9 for women following childbirth. (The overall annual suicide rate during the time of the study [1987 to 1994] was 11.3 per 100,000 women.) The authors concluded that induced abortion may have a harmful effect on mental health.[5]

Suicide is the ninth-ranking cause of all deaths in the United States[6] and the third-leading cause of death among young people fifteen to twenty-four years old. A 1991 study by the Centers for Disease Control and Prevention indicated that 27 percent of high school students have thought about suicide, 16 percent have had a plan, and 8 percent have made an attempt. Because stressful life events often trigger suicidal thoughts among teenagers, it is important for counselors and health care providers to exercise special vigilance when evaluating depressed or anxious adolescents after an abortion.

Re-Experiencing Events Related to the Abortion

Many post-abortion women are plagued by uncontrollable, painful memories that take the form of intrusive thoughts, dreams, or both. Everyone experiences persistent thoughts and flashback memories, both pleasant and unwelcome, from time to time. The smell of a certain aftershave may send a person back in time to an old relationship. Walking into Gramma's musty old house can trigger a multitude of childhood memories. A classic example of the more powerful waking flashback is the Vietnam veteran who dives for cover when a string of firecrackers explodes on the Fourth of July. In similar fashion, the post-abortion woman may experience distressing and intrusive flashbacks brought on by triggers such as the sound of a vacuum cleaner or the suction equipment in a dental office. Sometimes merely the aromas associated with a medical facility are enough to bring back unpleasant recollections.

Even more disturbing than waking flashbacks are nightmares. For the post-abortion woman these often involve recurring themes of lost, dismembered, or crying babies. They can be so grotesque and terrifying that she may awaken suddenly with a pounding heart, shakes, and an acute fear of returning to sleep. The following are some actual dreams that clients have described to me during therapy:

> I'm walking down the street and it's a beautiful day. Nothing is wrong at the beginning of the dream. The birds are singing and I am in a happy mood. Then a garbage truck passes me and stops at the house ahead of me. It empties a dumpster into the back of the truck, and as it starts to drive away I see a baby lying among the garbage that has just been emptied. She is screaming and holding her arms out to me. I know she wants me to

save her, because the crusher is about to come down and compact all the garbage. I am running after the truck but I can't catch up. She is about to be crushed, and then I wake up.

In my dream, I am awakened with a start because I know I have heard something. Then I hear it again. A tiny child is crying out, "Mommy, help me! Mommy, please come help me!" I look all over the room but can't find him. I hear him again. He is hanging by his little fingertips on the outside ledge of my third-story apartment window. I try to open the window to grab him, but it won't open. I look down at him and see that there is nothing below his waist—the lower half of his body has been hacked off and all of his blood is running out. He is dying and I can't save him.

It's something like the fairy tale of Rumpelstiltskin but more like a horror movie, with no little dwarf coming to help me. I am locked in a room, as big as a football field, that is filled with living baby parts—heads, arms, fingers, feet—and my "task" is to put all of these thousands of babies back together. I cannot do it. I sit down and weep because I know I will fail my task.

Both depression and nightmares may increase at the beginning of therapy or group work because of the need to focus on long-repressed material.

Fertility, Pregnancy, and Bonding Issues

It is not surprising that women who have lost a pregnancy, whether spontaneously or through abortion, may at some point experience some anxiety and conflict over issues related to childbearing in the future.

Preoccupation with becoming pregnant again. I've observed that a significant percentage of post-abortion women become pregnant within one year of their abortion. On the surface, one might assume that this is the result of an ongoing pattern of destructive relationships, damaged self-concept, immaturity, chaotic lifestyle, unwise choices, and failure to use contraception. But another explanation, one that often surfaces during counseling later in life, is the desire—usually not expressed openly, or even consciously—to create a baby that will replace the aborted child. Something seems to awaken within the soul of a woman who is pregnant, even though she may consciously reject any desire to have a baby at this time in her life. She is biologically primed to become a mother. I believe that when a woman's pregnancy is cut short (for any reason), there is a longing within her to become pregnant again, even if she may not have a logical reason to do so.

Sadly, but not surprisingly, this desire for a "replacement baby" often flies in the face of her circumstances. As a result, the same pressures that drove the first abortion are likely to lead to another. Currently in the United States, more than 40 percent of all abortions are performed on women who have already had at least one prior abortion.

Anxiety over fertility and childbearing issues. One of the potential complications of abortion is infertility or miscarriage of a pregnancy later in life. If a pelvic infection occurs in the wake of an abortion, the ensuing damage could prevent conception, interfere with the course of early pregnancy, or lead to ectopic pregnancy (a pregnancy that begins outside of the uterus and ultimately must be removed surgically). If the opening of the uterus (the cervix) is damaged during an abortion, it may become "incompetent" during a subsequent pregnancy, resulting in premature birth or miscarriage.

Women are supposed to be told of these and other potential risks before they undergo an abortion, but the quality of information given by abortion providers to women in crisis pregnancies has been a subject of some controversy over the years. Even when informed consent *is* given, for many women the details of possible problems in the future are lost in the heat of the moment. Needless to say, later in life when a pregnancy is truly desired, one or more abortions in the past can cast a long and worrisome shadow. Furthermore, even if an abortion is not a direct cause of infertility later in life, women who continue to be sexually active after an abortion (especially with multiple partners) may unknowingly acquire an infection that leads to pelvic inflammation and infertility. Few women are sadder than those who have aborted the only child(ren) they ever conceived.

The post-abortion woman with a religious worldview may be particularly susceptible to anxiety about future childbearing. If she believes that God is actively involved with individual human lives, she may fear that God will not allow her to become pregnant again, as a punishment for taking her baby's life. If she does become pregnant, she will imagine any number of gut-wrenching scenarios:

- the baby will be damaged prior to birth;
- the baby will be healthy but lost through miscarriage;
- the baby will be stillborn; or,
- she'll have a beautiful, healthy baby who will be taken from her during childhood.

Whatever the variation, the theme is always the same: "God will eventually punish me for having the abortion."

Interruption or disruption of the bonding process. Many post-abortion women experience distorted relationships with children, whether born before or after she had the abortion. This may manifest itself in two distinct ways.

I have seen some post-abortion women undertake a quest to become "The World's Most Perfect Mother." This is an unconscious (and often valiant) effort to prove to herself, to the world, and to God that she really *is* a good mother—even though she aborted one or more of her children. When finally given an opportunity to verbalize this belief, she may surprise herself by admitting that she hopes to distract God (or cosmic justice, karmic forces, or however else she might describe it) and forestall a disaster by doing a better-than-average job of protecting her child. This mom inevitably has a very tough time when her child hits adolescence and begins campaigning for independence. Often she will not be able to relax her grip and trust that her child will survive in the world without her protection.

The other type of disrupted relationship is more ominous, involving detachment or even devaluation of other children. Whether or not they harbor a fear of some form of divine retribution, many post-abortion women do not allow themselves to bond with another baby prior to birth for fear of experiencing loss. If she already has children at the time of the abortion, a woman may begin looking at them in a different light, unconsciously lowering their worth. A child who was once a priceless treasure, one to be guarded at all cost, may by degrees be downgraded to the status of a possession, one to be cherished—or thrown away—as circumstances dictate.

Tracy (whose story of a coerced abortion was told in the last chapter) was a woman whose two children were the focal point of her life. "I used to get up every morning thanking God that I could have such beautiful children. They were miracles to me. But now that I've had the abortion, I find myself sitting at the table watching them play and thinking crazy things like, 'Eeny, meeny, miney, mo, what if I had aborted *you?* Or *you?*' Suddenly they don't seem so special anymore, and I feel like I'm going nuts."

The most frightening consequence of interrupted bonding is the potential for child abuse. Canadian psychiatrist Philip Ney, M.D., has raised concerns about the worsening of child abuse statistics since the U.S. Supreme Court legalized abortion on demand in 1973:

> For over a decade those who wanted abortion on request argued that it was necessary for every child to be a wanted child. However, there are reasons to believe abortion on request not only has not solved the problem of unwanted, neglected, or battered children, it has worsened the problem. I have undertaken research on the subject on three continents over the past ten years using a variety of study populations. I've found a strong connection—almost causal connection—between child abuse and abortion.[7]

Survivor Guilt

In addition to experiencing guilt because they have violated their own moral code, many post-abortion women feel guilty because they are, in essence, the "survivor" of the abortion. In order to atone for what she perceives to be a profoundly selfish choice ("It's you or me, kid"), a woman may enter a self-sacrificing "compensation mode." She may keep herself busy doing volunteer work in the community, the church, or in pro-life or pro-choice organizations.[8] Some women even have a vague notion that a certain number of years of service—usually between five and seven—will somehow make up for the lost child.

Self-Abusive/Self-Destructive Behaviors

Compulsive and self-destructive behaviors are further symptoms of post-abortion distress.

Eating disorders. I believe that eating disorders arise in part from an unconscious desire to become less of a sexual target (and in so doing to reduce the odds of becoming pregnant again) through substantial weight loss or gain. The most prevalent expression is a drift to the overweight end of the spectrum, but anorexia is also common. (In extreme cases, anorexia causes an interruption of menstrual cycles, thus ensuring that another pregnancy cannot begin.)

Alcohol or other substance abuse. The Elliott Institute, a research organization based in Virginia, studied the reproductive history of 700 women randomly selected from a national survey. They found that women who aborted their first pregnancy were 3.9 times more likely to engage in subsequent drug or alcohol abuse than those who had never had an abortion.[9] One could argue that alcohol and drug abusers are more likely to exercise poor judgment while "under the influence," and thus are more at risk for unplanned pregnancies, which are subsequently aborted. But my experience with post-abortion women has also convinced me that alcohol and other substances are used by many to reduce the intensity of grief and anxiety following the abortion. Unfortunately, drugs and alcohol not only bring their own measure of destruction and grief, but also postpone (or even prevent) the bereavement process that is necessary to bring resolution to the pain.

Cigarette smoking. A number of research studies have documented increased tobacco use among women who have a history of one or more abortions. More ominous is the finding that women who have had an abortion are more likely to smoke during subsequent pregnancies that they carry to term. A four-year study in Washington state found that 18 percent of women who had never had an abortion smoked while pregnant, compared with 28 percent of those who had had one previous abortion, 31 percent of those who had had two abortions, and 41.6 percent of those who had had four or more abortions.[10]

A pregnancy is one of the few events in life that consistently induces habitual tobacco users to quit (at least until the baby is born), as the instinct to defend one's preborn child overrides the powerful urge to smoke. A woman's willingness to quit smoking during pregnancy appears to decrease dramatically if she has had one or more prior abortions. This lends support to the notion that abortion disrupts maternal instincts.

Other self-punishing or self-degrading behaviors. I have observed other behaviors that suggest that self-concept deteriorates among women with unresolved issues related to an abortion decision. Some women enter into abusive relationships or become promiscuous (though this behavior may also be fallout from abusive sexual experiences earlier in life, especially during childhood). Some fail to take care of basic medical needs or even attempt to hurt themselves physically. Saundra was like that.

Saundra had her first abortion when she was sixteen. She was brokenhearted when her boyfriend broke up with her shortly after taking her to the clinic. Lacking friends with whom she could commiserate, she looked for comfort in another relationship, which quickly became sexual. She married at eighteen, and before long her husband became verbally and then physically abusive. After one particularly severe beating four years later, Saundra finally left him. She was barely able to live on the tips she collected as a cocktail waitress. She called me for a counseling appointment because she had begun cutting herself in an effort to "feel alive."

I never cease to be dismayed by the fact that the women who most desperately need consoling and nurturing are so often the ones least equipped with a healthy understanding of how to care for themselves.

Anniversary Reactions

Around the time of the anniversary of the abortion, the due date of the aborted child, or both, a significant number of women will have increasingly distressing symptoms.

Tanya aborted twins on a cold, blustery October morning more than two decades ago. The episode was so incredibly painful for her that she moved to Southern California to start a new life. She eventually met a wonderful man, married him, and had a baby. Overall she was happy beyond measure, but she couldn't understand why she became depressed, withdrawn, and physically sick every October. She never connected this annual slump to the previous abortion because she had "forgotten" the date of the procedure. It wasn't until she began participating in a post-abortion therapy group and deliberately revisited the details of her experience, that she remembered the exact date of her abortion and recognized its significance. It has been eight years since she worked through her post-abortion issues, and she has yet to experience another depression or illness in October.

Brief Psychotic Disorder

Rarely, a post-abortion woman will experience a

brief psychotic episode, during which her perception of reality becomes drastically distorted. This break with reality occurs within two weeks of the abortion and lasts a very short period of time (less than twenty-four hours), after which she returns to her previous level of functioning. While this is a very uncommon reaction to abortion, it bears mentioning because it is possible for a person to have a brief psychotic reaction to a stressful event without a previous history of psychotic reactions or subsequent episodes.

I have personally worked with a client who experienced a brief psychosis immediately after her abortion. This respected professional lived by herself in a small town. She passed a very large piece of bloody material only hours after returning home from an abortion clinic. She examined it and concluded that it was her eight-week fetus. The clinic had been extremely busy on the day of her procedure. She believed that the physician neglected to confirm that the fetus had passed through the suction tube or perhaps she had been carrying twins. She was shocked and horrified by the unmistakably human appearance of what lay before her.

She carefully wrapped the bloody tissue in a soft kitchen towel, decided that it was a girl, gave her a name, and rocked and talked to her for the next several hours. When she awakened the next morning with the fetus (still wrapped in the towel) lying in her bed, she understood that she had had a break from reality. She then drove to a nearby beach because she wanted to bury her baby in the ocean. Needless to say, she was badly shaken by the experience. She returned to the abortion clinic Monday morning, where the staff informed her that she must have imagined the entire episode. Having seen newspaper advertising for post-abortion counseling at a local Crisis Pregnancy Center, she came for help soon thereafter.

By the time a post-abortion woman is experiencing several of these symptoms (especially guilt and depression) her defenses against the emotional pain are being stripped away. She is at the point where the grieving process for the decision and the lost child can begin.

Chapter Three

Beginning to Grieve

❖ ❖ ❖ ❖ ❖ ❖

Consider the experience of a woman whose two-year-old has just died as the result of an accident or a serious illness. She will, with rare exception, not only be surrounded by attentive loved ones and friends, but will also receive offers of help with food, housework, and child care if she has other children. There will be a memorial service, attended by comforters from near and far, during which the child's short life will be celebrated. She will have memories of the pregnancy, childbirth, and two birthday celebrations. She will have dozens of pictures (and probably videos as well) of her toddler, and a dresser full of tiny clothes that still hold the child's fragrance. In most communities she will have access to support groups and individual counseling to help her work through the stages of her grief. And, when she needs to do so, she can sit by a gravestone that has been erected over the body of a child whose life and passing were acknowledged and honored.

By contrast, in our society a pregnancy loss—a profound event in a woman's life—is poorly understood and often not recognized as worthy of being mourned. Some will perhaps attend a memorial service for a stillborn child, but this is usually more of a dutiful courtesy to the parents than a genuine recognition of the loss of a "real" human being. If a woman miscarries at five or six months, however, little if any thought is given to commemorating the baby's brief and unseen life. His or her mother must grieve alone, perhaps joined (for a while) by a husband who may or may not understand the gravity of her loss, or perhaps by a friend who has had a similar experience.

If these pregnancy losses are rarely deemed worthy of a formal leave-taking ritual in our culture, there is certainly no recognition of the need to grieve the loss of a baby by abortion. Not only is the status and value of a preborn human still hotly contested in the legal, medical, and political arenas, but the woman's right to end her pregnancy is widely considered to be a constitutional prerogative on a par with freedom of speech or religious expression. So if a woman chooses to have an abortion in order to bring a personal crisis to an end, why on earth should she be upset about losing her baby? Needless to say, the post-abortion woman faces a number of monumental barriers to moving through the process of grieving her loss or even recognizing that she has experienced a loss at all:

> ✧ **There is no external evidence that her baby ever existed.** There are no baby pictures or other memorabilia. Whatever memories she carries are linked primarily to the tumult created by the crisis preg-

nancy and the abortion experience. If she saw her baby at all, her memories may be horrific ones of deformity, dismemberment, and death.

✧ **The post-abortion woman usually believes that she has no right to grieve a loss that she herself has chosen.** She may, of course, identify the situation leading to the abortion as a cause for grief (especially if the sexual encounter involved coercion or poor judgment on her part). She may also feel drained or even traumatized by the procedure and its discomforts. But since losing the baby was the sole purpose of the procedure, it doesn't seem reasonable to grieve that loss as well.

✧ **There is no public forum for grieving the loss of her child.** A healthy grieving process includes an occasion, whether formal and ceremonial (such as a memorial service) or informal (such as swapping stories at a wake), which serves to acknowledge the significance of the loved one who is gone. But who organizes a ceremony for an aborted fetus? And if there were a service, who would the post-abortion woman invite? Who would give a eulogy, and what would he or she say?

✧ **The support system that usually gathers around a bereaved mother is very limited, or absent altogether, for the post-abortion woman.** In most cases few people are even told about the abortion. She may be brought to the clinic by a confidant and then taken home to guard her secret from unsuspecting family members. No one will likely offer to bring her meals or run errands for her. After all, abortion isn't supposed to be a big deal from a medical or emotional perspective, and the vast majority of women having abortions are young and in good health. This isn't exactly a broken hip or cancer surgery. Who would anticipate the need for help with recovery?

Furthermore, the very people who supported a woman's abortion decision aren't likely to be excited about rehashing it afterward—even though that is precisely what someone who has suffered a loss usually feels compelled to do. Since there appears to be no legitimate need for a grieving process, even time-tested confidants may tire of hearing what seems like an endless stream of moaning and groaning about the abortion, or they may erroneously believe that it is unhealthy to dwell on it.

❖ **If a post-abortion woman's need to process her experience leads her to confide in someone who did *not* know about the abortion, she risks an unpredictable reaction.** Even a close friend or family member may respond with disapproval or even anger, a devastating confirmation that the woman must be beyond redemption. In the wake of such rejection, she is not likely to reach out for an understanding ear again.

✧ **The preparation for the abortion rarely includes any discussion of the possibility of emotional issues—especially grieving—afterwards.** As I have already mentioned, most abortion clinics are weak in the area of informed consent—especially information about possible negative emotional effects of abortion. If a woman goes back to the clinic to verbalize her emotional confusion ("Why am I feeling so depressed and guilty about this?"), she will probably be told that her feelings are the product of shifting hormones and will soon disappear on their own.

✧ **If she is troubled enough by feelings of distress after an abortion a woman may seek help from a counselor who may—but more likely may not—recognize her need to work through the appropriate stages of grieving.** The counselor may gloss over the idea that the abortion could represent a significant loss, encouraging her to look instead for the *real* source of her pain. This message from "The Professional" that the abortion should not be causing such a disturbance effectively derails the grieving process.

For all of these reasons, the post-abortion woman

is often left without any validation of her feelings and as a result she may repress them. Without an opportunity to work through it, the grieving process is interrupted and may not be resumed until years later, when another significant loss occurs. This may trigger a response whose magnitude and intensity seem out of proportion to the present loss and often out of control as well. *Why am I having such a horrible reaction to this? Am I losing my grip?* A therapist may help the woman dig backward to seek other unresolved episodes similar to the one currently "on the plate." The present trauma cannot be successfully resolved until older traumas are finally identified and worked through.

The Five Phases of Grieving an Abortion

Just as the process of grieving any type of loss can vary greatly among individuals, even within a homogeneous cultural environment, the look and sound of each post-abortion woman's grief will also be quite unique. In fact, depending upon timing and current circumstances, some may not appear to manifest any grief at all. Nevertheless, the majority of women who have had an abortion at some point experience at least the first two of the following phases. Many appear to settle in the second phase (numbing) and never move past it.

Phase one: Shock and intense emotion

In the normal grieving process, a person reacts to

the loss of someone (or something) specific, identifiable, and usually widely recognized as valuable—a loved one, a marriage, a home, a job, a competition, even a pet. But the post-abortion woman has major barriers to identifying her loss as authentic and so she is often stunned and confused when she experiences unpleasant feelings, whether immediately or in the distant future. She is relieved that the crisis is over, but also bewildered by the intensity of the pain she is feeling and the lack of a meaningful road map to navigate through it. *(I thought this was just a simple procedure, and that I would feel fine when it was all over.)* She needs to revisit her decision to abort but no one wants to listen to her talk about it.

If she does not find someone to help her walk through this phase of the grieving process, which can last anywhere from a few days to a few weeks, in most cases defense mechanisms will quietly take charge of the situation, in order to protect her sanity.

Phase two: Numbing

No one can live with raw, smarting emotions indefinitely. If they can't be healed, they need to be anesthetized. The process begins with a list of internal "rules":

> Don't talk about the abortion procedure.
> Don't talk about your feelings.
> If someone—even a doctor—asks if you've
> had an abortion, say "No."
> Drugs and alcohol can bring relief.

Fill your life with a lot of other activities.

Avoid conversations with people about abortion.

Avoid films and TV programs that have anything to do with pregnancy, birth, and especially abortion.

Don't take a position in the pro-life/prochoice debate; or,

Take a hard-line position on one side or the other of the debate.

Deny any grief, or any feelings at all, about the loss of your unborn child through abortion.

Hold back from grieving other losses, especially those involving death.

Deny any connection between other problems in life and the abortion.

This phase can last anywhere from a few months to several years, often with profoundly negative effects in a woman's life. (I've talked to women who weren't able to move past it for fifty years after an abortion.) In a "healthy" post-abortion grieving process, this phase would ideally be eliminated, or shortened as much as possible.

Phase three: Disorganization and depression

The work required to push away negative thoughts about the abortion consumes an enormous amount of emotional energy. If a post-abortion woman reaches a place in her life where stresses are piling up, her defense mechanisms will begin to crumble. Unwanted thoughts about the abortion will storm the mental breech, and jumbled images of all of the losses in her life may join them. If this continues, she may sink into despair about her life in general. Hopefully, her depression will drive her to reach out to friends, clergy, and/or a professional counselor in the effort to regain control over a life that seems literally to be falling apart.

Phase four: Mourning and healing

Healing begins with a very uncomfortable process—facing the shame and guilt felt about the abortion. This is the long-avoided opening of the emotional boil, and what pours out can be intensely unpleasant and, in some cases, even self-destructive:

- ◆ "I killed my child—it wasn't just a mass of tissue."
- ◆ "I'm selfish and self-centered, and I hate myself."
- ◆ "I will never be able to forgive myself or receive forgiveness for the abortion."
- ◆ "I hate everyone who had a part in the abortion decision."
- ◆ "I should hurt the rest of my life for what I have done."

Having acknowledged these feelings, if she has the proper guidance (whether through a book, support group, or counselor), she is now ready to move through the healing stages. Because she is no longer using coping strategies to deny her feelings and personal responsibility for her choice, she can begin working through and resolving her guilt, anger, and grief. (This process is described in detail in the next several chapters.)

Phase five: Reintegration and adaptation

If she successfully works through the healing process, a woman is now released from the debilitating stranglehold of guilt, anger, and grief. Her statements about herself are markedly different:

- ◆ "I acknowledge what I have done."
- ◆ "Life was taken; my baby died as a result of my decisions. But I have asked for and known God's forgiveness, and can go forward with my life."
- ◆ "I am again able to feel sadness and joy. I am no longer emotionally numb."
- ◆ "I am not a 'lesser' human being any more."
- ◆ "I can share my experiences with others."

The healing process brings re-integration to the post-abortion woman. She no longer must compartmentalize her life or push the abortion experience and its fallout into the recesses of her mind. Everything is exposed, and what has been exposed is healed. She can speak with other women who have had abortions, return to emotional intimacy, and allow herself to experience the joy of spiritual awakening. Self-destructive behaviors are replaced with behaviors that reinforce her value.

Charlotte's Story

Charlotte, twenty-five, discovered that she was pregnant in February and opted to have an abortion, not only to prevent the derailment of her career but also to preserve what had appeared to be a promising relationship. A few weeks after the abortion she made an appointment to see me. She was astonished by the chaos of negative emotions she was experiencing. She was having trouble concentrating on her demanding work assignments. The man in her life had abruptly decided to seek romantic fulfillment elsewhere. The friends who had told her that an abortion was the only sensible decision no longer wanted to listen to her outpouring of grief.

I met with Charlotte for three months, but as we continued I developed a feeling that we were spinning our wheels. Every week she would repeat her litany of anger and grief and I would listen sympathetically, but she was unable to work successfully through any of her issues. By June, after more than twelve sessions, Charlotte was beginning to cancel appointments. I was on the verge of suggesting that we take a break and resume in September, but I knew she was far from being ready to stop therapy. She was barely holding on to her job and had increasingly isolated herself.

When she neglected to reschedule the most recently skipped appointment, I called and left a message, but she didn't return my call. I left another message telling her I understood how difficult it was to address her abortion pain, and that I was eager to continue meeting with her whenever she was ready. I didn't hear from Charlotte until many months later. She was experiencing an overt clinical depression and had seen a psychiatrist who had prescribed antidepressant and anti-anxiety medications, and also recommended that she continue therapy.

Charlotte and I met from September through the following February, diligently and painfully working our way along her healing path. As our time together drew to a close, Charlotte was a different person. She was making steady progress through her grief and was finding spiritual and emotional healing.

Experiencing healing from a profound loss does not imply that grief will never again be experienced. The post-abortion woman will still weep on the anniversary date of the abortion, observe quietly the birthdays her child would have had, and wonder what he or she would have looked like. There will still be regret for the choice. But healing *does* mean that the abortion will never again have the power to oppress her life and relationships.

Part Two

The Healing Journey

❖ ❖ ❖ ❖ ❖ ❖

The next few chapters of this book will describe a process of healing and restoration that has been successfully completed by thousands of post-abortion women. In order to give a sense of the flesh-and-blood struggle that I have observed at close range, this section will follow four very real women whom I have gathered together in a composite support group. While their names and some details have been altered to protect their anonymity, I have worked with each of them—I call them Cassandra, Jenny, Cindy, and Shana.

Chapter Four

Facing the Past

❖ ❖ ❖ ❖ ❖ ❖

It was the first night of the support group. The ground rules had been set and confidentiality assured. In a brief opening round, each of the four women stated how she felt about being in the group. Then I asked each person to share some basic information about her abortion experience if she was comfortable doing so. There was a nervous silence in the room. Finally, one brave soul began.

Cassandra: Well, my first abortion was about twelve years ago. I was seventeen years old, and I had been with my boyfriend for almost a year. I guess you could say he was my first true love. I think I was about three months along—I can't remember exactly. Sam convinced me that we couldn't have a baby during our senior year of high school. And it didn't take much convincing; I was so scared my parents would find out. Sam made all the arrangements and took me to the clinic. We broke up a couple of weeks later. My second abortion happened in college. It was just kind of a fleeting thing with this guy, and I had the abortion very early in the pregnancy. The student health service took care of everything. That one doesn't bother me nearly as much as the first one. I've been married to Tom now for three years, but he doesn't know about either abortion.

Teri: Where does he think you are tonight?

Cassandra: I told him I was starting a cooking class! I really think he would think badly of me if I told him. Probably for not telling him earlier more than for the abortions themselves.

Teri: What made you decide to not tell him when you were dating?

Cassandra: Tom comes from a very *Leave It to Beaver* kind of family. I wanted to tell him, but the more deeply I got into the relationship, the more scared I became of what his reaction might be, so I just never got around to telling him. I think I was hoping it would just sort of go away if I didn't ever talk about it again. But since the birth of our daughter last year, I can't stop thinking about the two children I aborted.

Jenny: I need to tell you, Cassandra, that I'm so glad you went first and said you had two abortions, because I've had three, and my greatest fear about coming to this group was that I would be the only one who's had more than one abortion. The first one was when I was fourteen. I was in the eighth grade. It's funny, because I remember a lot about that one, but the details on the other two are very fuzzy. Anyway, I was so naive that I didn't even know I was pregnant until I was almost four months along. I had only started having periods a year earlier, and they hadn't become regular yet, so I didn't realize that I had missed one. My boyfriend was also in the eighth grade. He said he would get the money for an abortion but by the time it dawned on me that he wasn't going to come through, I was five months along. I finally told my mom. She was furious. My older sister had had a baby out of wedlock, and my mom said she wasn't going to go through that again. She made all the arrangements, and I had a saline abortion in some hospital. It was pretty bad. I cried all the way home and mom didn't say a thing because she was so mad. We never talked about it again. When I got pregnant a couple of years later, I just took care of it myself and Mom never knew. The last one was sometime during my early twenties. I feel so stupid for not being able to remember. The period of my life between about fifteen to twenty-five is actually pretty much a blur for me.

Teri: It's not uncommon to have fuzzy memories about a period of your life that was traumatic for you. Did you go to college?

Jenny: Are you kidding? It's a miracle that I got out of high school! I was a pretty wild kid, and they put me into a continuation school. I finally finished. I tried taking a couple of classes at a local junior college, but it just wasn't for me. And besides, I couldn't wait to get out of the house, which meant I had to work full-time. I bounced around from one rental situation to another. It was pretty chaotic. I think I moved two or three times a year until I was twenty-five. Then I met my first husband. He looked like a meal ticket to me and when he proposed I jumped at the chance. It only lasted a year. I've been married three times altogether. The second one was a doozy, and now I'm separated from my third husband. I've been living at my mom's for six months.

Teri: Does she know you're attending this group?

Jenny: Yeah. She didn't say much about it one way or another. Like I said, we've never talked about that first abortion. I wonder sometimes if she ever thinks about it. I wonder if she ever regrets it. I'm not counting on a chance to talk to her about it. You could call my mother Cleopatra—the queen of denial!

Cindy: I'll go next. I had an abortion eleven years ago. I was twenty-two. But I'm a little confused because I don't think I'm feeling as bad as I should. I mean, obviously I felt the need to come in the first place. I thought this would be more traumatic, since I've never told anybody about my abortion. So I'm really surprised at how blank I feel right now. Does this mean I shouldn't be in the group?

Teri: Not necessarily, Cindy, although you always have the freedom to leave if you're not comfortable. I've heard similar feelings from many women during the first meeting. Being emotional is not a requirement to be here. Everyone's path to healing is different and you can go at your own speed. Don't compare yourself with anyone else in the group. Just do the work and see where the healing process takes you, okay?

Cindy: This won't take long. I had just graduated

from college, found a great job with a prestigious company, and had started working on my M.B.A. It was a really hectic time in my life. I was dating Bill, who is my husband now. When we found out I was pregnant, the decision wasn't difficult at all. We were both in total agreement that I should have an abortion. I was eight weeks along. Everything went smoothly—there wasn't anything traumatic about it. Bill and I had already talked about getting married within a couple of years, and I guess I just figured there would be more pregnancies in the future after our careers were firmly launched. We got married right on schedule, and everything was perfect. We were the ultimate yuppies! When I turned thirty, we had been married for six years and the old biological clock began ticking very loudly. We've been trying for three years now, and the bills from the infertility workup are really starting to pile up, but we haven't had any luck so far. It's been pretty rocky at home for a while. I guess I called about being in the group because I'm beginning to think that I aborted the only pregnancy I'm ever going to have, and it's freaking me out. [Tears well up in her eyes.] Well! Maybe I'm a little emotional about this after all!

Bill knows I'm attending this group and he's not a happy camper. He can't imagine why on earth I would want to dredge up ancient history like this. But then he hasn't been happy about much of anything for the past few months.

Teri: Do you think it's possible that he feels a little nervous about you looking at something he's not ready to deal with yet?

Cindy: I hadn't thought about it that way, but you may be right. I don't know. It's hard to tell because we just haven't been talking very much.

Teri: Shana, would you like to share tonight?

Shana: I had my abortion three years ago. We have four other children and we assumed we were done. I was forty-one when I got pregnant, and it was a total shock since our youngest was almost through grade school at that point. My doctor urged me to let him do the abortion. He said the risk for a fetal defect was too high. My husband didn't want the abortion, but I was so tired of raising children. The four kids came pretty close together. I just went ahead and did it, and my husband's never forgiven me. He says he has, but it's just not the same between us anymore.

My other children don't know about the pregnancy. I had the abortion quite early. For a while, I thought John was so angry that he was going to tell them just to punish me. But he didn't. I don't think I regret the abortion itself, but I feel very badly about the effect it's had on our marriage. I had no idea that John would take it so hard. I feel betrayed by my doctor. He was my OB for all four of the children, and I trusted him. I didn't even think twice about having the abortion because he was so definite about it being the right thing to do. He even knew that John was opposed to it. I don't think I would have had the abortion if he hadn't been so persuasive. I've actually switched to another doctor now. And I think that's all I want to share for now, if you guys don't mind.

❖ ❖ ❖ ❖ ❖ ❖

The first step in the healing journey is peeling away the callus formed by months and years of denying and suppressing the painful emotions connected with the abortion experience. Why is it necessary to dredge up that which the mind has worked so hard to forget? Because the grief, anger, and guilt a woman felt about the events surrounding her abortion were never processed. They were bundled up and hidden away because they were too painful to deal with, but they continue to fester like an untreated infection.

When the mind pushes down unwanted emotions connected to a past trauma, the bad *feelings* are the first to be packed away. If that isn't enough to bring some relief, the actual *facts* surrounding the event may be suppressed as well. Details about events before, during, and after the episode may be lost from memory.

When a woman's symptoms become so uncomfortable that she is ready to talk about a previous abortion, it is common for her to experience a frustrating inability to remember much about it. She may desire to remember long-forgotten feelings and details, but she tells her story in a detached, clinical fashion—as if she is describing a stranger's experience.

Total recall usually does not occur in a sudden flash. Memories come to the surface a few at a time, as the mind deems it safe to handle them. When a woman first tells her abortion story (usually with considerable apprehension) and finds the therapist or support group members to be compassionate and nonjudgmental, she is likely to return to the next session surprised by the amount of detail she was able to remember during the week between appointments. In fact, I have seen women return to the second or third session very shaken because they have suddenly remembered one or more additional abortions that they had completely blocked from memory. Less dramatic (and much more common) is the emergence of specific details that had long been forgotten: the name of the clinic, details of the procedure, how far the pregnancy had pro-gressed, and so forth.

Sometimes a post-abortion woman who *wants* to cooperate with the healing process becomes frustrated because she simply cannot remember much of what happened to her. Since all of the five senses create memories, it is often helpful to revisit the experience while someone asks ques-tions. Just as the scent of a cologne worn by an old boyfriend can suddenly provoke a flood of memories about that relationship, so her recollec-tion of the events surrounding the abortion can be quickened by thinking about not only sights and sounds but smell and touch as well.

Remembrance comes in layers and at differ-ent speeds for every woman. One who had an abortion a year ago still has access to many de-tails, but it is usually much harder for women who have had an abortion several years ago. In order to make progress in the healing process, it is actually not necessary for her to remember *everything* about her abortion but only enough to get at negative feelings associated with it. When I run a group, there is always at least one woman who will become frustrated with herself for not remembering as "fast" as the others. Remembrance cannot be forced! I always encourage that woman simply to work with what is in front of her. What needs to come will come. I never operate under the delusion that I can somehow "break" a person's denial system. Confrontation or manipulation will only elicit a hostile or defensive response. And if there simply are not many negative emotions for her to deal with, I don't want to be responsible for creating false memories or feelings for her.

The abortion wound

Most post-abortion women carry an "abortion wound" in their hearts but have never specifically identified it or understood its ongoing impact. During this step of the healing process it is often helpful to work with a visual image. A woman can describe what her abortion wound looks like, how it feels, and how it has affected her life. She might draw the wound or make a descriptive collage using pictures from a stack of magazines. Here are examples of what women have described:

A broken teacup
A dark hole that admits no light
A small cage
A black heart wrapped in a strong chain

Some have a difficult time thinking in pictures, and I will ask them to come up with words that might symbolize their pain (or to cut words from magazines). This visual picture of the wound serves as a benchmark at the end of our time together and helps the woman understand how far she has come in her healing journey.

Journaling

Many women find it valuable to begin the remembrance process by writing answers to the questions in a journal. The following list is by no means complete, and I encourage each woman to add her own questions and responses as they occur to her.

1. How did you meet the father of the baby?
2. At the time you decided to have sex with him, what was your understanding about the relationship? What do you think was his understanding of the relationship?
3. Did you ever talk together about the possibility of your sexual activity leading to pregnancy? Was there a mutual understanding as to what course of action would be taken if you became pregnant?
4. What did you feel when you first found out you were pregnant?
5. What was your boyfriend's/husband's reaction? Friends' reactions? Parents' reactions? What did they want you to do?
6. What were your feelings about abortion before your pregnancy? Was your decision to

abort a violation of your internal code of right and wrong?
7. How did you get to the abortion clinic? How did you feel as you were driving/riding there? What was said? What do you wish had been said?
8. What was it like in the waiting room? Describe the atmosphere around you. What did the other patients seem to be feeling?
9. What did the table feel like? What was going through your mind? Did you have second thoughts?
10. How would you describe the clinic workers? Were they understanding and sympathetic? What did you need that they didn't or couldn't provide?
11. How did you feel—physically and emotionally—while the abortion was being performed? What did you see? Hear? Smell?
12. How did you feel—physically and emotionally—when it was over?
13. After the abortion, what happened to your relationship with your boyfriend/husband? With your parents? With any friend(s) who had an important vote in your abortion decision?
14. What do you feel has been the most detrimental effect of the abortion on your life?
15. If you were in similar circumstances today, would you make the same choice?

A woman may answer these questions in a superficial way when she first works through them. The mind's capacity to avoid confronting uncomfortable information is very well developed, and it may take a few attempts to uncover the old feelings. If this occurs, I encourage her to put her answers away for a few days and then try again. The material she is looking for eventually becomes more accessible as a result of her first efforts.

Chapter Five

Guilt and Forgiveness

❖ ❖ ❖ ❖ ❖ ❖

In preparation for this session, the women completed a journaling exercise called "Created for Love" that is designed to help an individual take an inventory of her thoughts about spiritual issues. (This exercise is reproduced in appendix 2.) I asked the women how they felt about the journaling project.

Cassandra: I felt kind of curious and maybe a little excited. I had no religious training whatsoever growing up, and I've actually not thought a whole lot about whether there's life after death, punishment and reward, a God. So for me, the journaling questions were very thought provoking.

Shana: I'll be honest and say that the homework seemed like a waste of time to me. I don't want to insult anyone here who is religious, but I just don't understand how any human being can ever say "Oh yes, such and such is definitely the truth" when there is absolutely no way to prove that there is anything after death. So why spend time debating it?

I'm Jewish, but growing up we never went to synagogue unless my mom's parents were visiting. They were very religious. When the subject did come up, my parents pretty much told me I was free to figure this stuff out on my own. I went through a stage during the late seventies when I looked into all kinds of world religions, but nothing hung together for me.

It doesn't bother me if you all need to talk about it. I can't be sure there *isn't* anything out there, you know? I really feel okay if other people have strong religious persuasions, because I could be wrong. I just hated growing up with my grandmother always nudging me about going to synagogue and claiming my Jewish heritage and all that.

Jenny: That's just how I feel, too. I grew up in a really rigid Christian home. I'm talking about church four or five times a week. But I didn't see that it made any difference in my parents' lives. So I walked away from it all by the time I was old enough to think for myself. It's funny. I haven't logged any time thinking about all this for years, but when I did this stupid project, I was surprised to learn that I do still believe there's a God. I didn't realize that I was actually really hacked off at him! I think I'm really angry at him for not protecting me from all the bad things that have happened in my life. Where *was* he during my abortions and lousy marriages? Why didn't he stop me? I don't like what this has stirred up in me. Part of me wants to keep pretending that I have no interest in thinking about this stuff, and part of me understands that my anger toward God goes so deep inside of me that it is somehow foundational.

Cindy: I think my response to the project was a little different. I was raised Catholic and still attend Mass regularly. And I'm not offended by what anyone has said. I think I have a lot of *fear* toward God, but it would never occur to me to be *angry* with him. That's just unthinkable! All I feel is an overwhelming guilt for the abortion. I feel like I'm just trying to steer clear of God—not get on his radar. As it is, I feel like he's punishing me by not letting me get pregnant for the past three years.

From the Bible I know that David was plenty ticked lots of times and didn't mind telling God. But somehow in my mind it was okay for him to yell at God because they were real close, so God would put up with a lot from him. If I think of me saying those kinds of things to God, I picture him turning around, looking at me and saying, "Excuse me, are you talking to me, regular person? Do I even know you—have we met?"

Of course, that doesn't line up at all with my Catholic beliefs. That's why I'm miserable. That's why I choose not to think too hard about this kind of stuff. It doesn't add up, and so I feel like a hypocrite.

❖ ❖ ❖ ❖ ❖ ❖

When I ask post-abortion women to look at spiritual issues in most cases, I am not bringing up anything that hasn't already been the source of a lot of middle-of-the-night anxiety. I'm merely providing a safe, nonjudgmental place for them to verbalize the pain that most of them are already experiencing. Typically, a post-abortion woman has never had the opportunity to verbalize her thoughts about God and her abortion. When given the occasion, she may be surprised at what flows freely out of her mouth.

Most people have some sort of concept of God and an afterlife, even though the descriptions they might offer differ widely. In fact, I never cease to be impressed by the eagerness of clients in counseling, or women in a post-abortion support group, to discuss spiritual issues—even if they've rarely (or never) talked about them before. I have concluded that only a small percentage of people is actually willing to believe that existence stops with the last breath. The old adage that "there are no atheists in a foxhole" certainly holds true for most people who are in crisis. When distress brings the flow of life to a crushing halt, issues that are easily shoved aside during everyday tasks suddenly come up for review and analysis, including spiritual issues—issues such as:

◆ Is there life after death?
◆ Is there a God who knows me individually?
◆ Did my baby have a soul? If so, where is my baby now?
◆ If my baby is conscious somewhere in the afterlife, does he or she hate me now?
◆ Will I meet my baby when I die?
◆ If my baby is with God, and I'm the one who ended his or her life, will I be able to be with God after I die? Do I even *want* to be wherever God and my baby are?
◆ How angry is God with me for the abortion? Am I in store for divine punishment?

Most post-abortion women find these questions

too painful to contemplate because there doesn't seem to be any happy ending that they can anticipate after this life ends. They will tend to push these thoughts to a very distant back burner. When they do formulate some provisional answers to these questions, the answers tend to run like this: "Yes, there is a God and he knows I had an abortion. I have forfeited any chance of being in relationship with him. In fact, I am unredeemable. Yes, I know that God's forgiveness is supposed to be available to everyone, but I simply do not believe God forgives a mother who ends the life of her own child. I expect to be forever banished from God's good graces. I will never be blessed for the rest of my life, and I deserve any and all bad things that happen to me. If by some miracle I *do* manage to get into heaven, I'll be residing with those who just barely made it. No doubt it will be because we managed to say the right prayers and go through the right rituals, so that God has no choice but (begrudgingly) to take us in."

This painful experience in her life offers the woman a chance to discover and perhaps redefine her concept of God. I believe that for a woman who acknowledges the existence of a personal God, long-term healing will come only when she asks for total and unconditional forgiveness.

Ironically, the woman with a Judeo-Christian orientation often has a difficult time accepting God's forgiveness for her abortion. If feelings of closeness to God were enjoyed prior to the abortion, few (if any) such feelings exist afterwards, and she will probably feel that the rift in the relationship is irreparable. Many women cannot tolerate these feelings for long and will seek relief by turning away from any involvement in church or synagogue whatsoever. Others enter into an intense compensation mode, assuming that if they are "good" long enough, if they "prove themselves," God might forgive them some day. This is rarely a conscious thought process, however. During therapy a woman may startle herself by realizing that she has actually formulated a specific number of years (usually five to seven) as a sufficient period of penance. ("If I keep a spotless record for a few years, hopefully God will review my case and show a little mercy.") As is true of so many issues in healing the emotions, bringing these unconscious beliefs into consciousness is vital, so that they might be first understood and then appropriately revised.

Three Aspects of Forgiveness

Even if we were raised without formal religious training, we have grown up in a society that is, for the most part, Judeo-Christian in heritage. As a result, some basic concepts about God, right and wrong, and life after death are usually part of our lives, whether or not we have spent much time in church.[1]

So how will the Christian woman view her post-abortion relationship to God? My clients often can recite a Bible verse or catechism learned during childhood. They describe God not only as

the Creator of the universe but also as the perfect, loving parent who desires a deep and abiding relationship with those whom he has created.
But he also made us with the ability to choose
whether or not we will have any relationship with
him. Our relationship with God has been disrupted by our tendency to ignore him—living as
though he doesn't exist at all—or engaging in
outright rebellion, whether sporadically or as a
lifelong pursuit. Our relationship with him will be
re-established only when God offers and we accept
forgiveness for our countless violations of God's law.
But God is offering us such forgiveness.

Yet many post-abortion women are secretly
convinced that their transgressions are beyond
the reach of God's forgiveness. Their most important task, then, is to accept on an emotional level
what they may already know on an intellectual
level: that God's forgiveness is available and that
they must decide to reach out and grasp it.
There are three important aspects to this "firm
grasp" on forgiveness: knowing who ultimately
has paid the debt for their wrongdoing, allowing
intimacy with God to be restored, and understanding the difference between punishment and
consequences.

Debt paid in full

I love Jesus' story of the ungrateful servant in the
New Testament (Matthew 18). In this parable, a
servant asked his master for time to pay back a
huge debt. The debt equaled far more than the
servant's entire lifetime earning potential. Seeing

the servant's acute anxiety, the master told the servant that he forgave the entire debt. Shortly thereafter, the servant came across someone who owed him a very small amount. The servant tried to shake the debt out of the man who owed it. This story illustrates the importance of forgiving others in small matters when we have been forgiven in enormous ones.

Whenever I hear this parable, I can't help entertaining a little different take on the story, inspired by the women I have met who are still trying to work off their "debt." I imagine the servant being so panicked and preoccupied with paying his impossible debt that he doesn't even hear the master or comprehend what has happened. And so, in his frantic effort to raise money, he accosts the first person who owes him something, an act that is not only hurtful but also unnecessary.

Believers know that God has made provision for the forgiving of wrongdoing. But many women have a difficult time believing that forgiveness is available for their selfish and catastrophic choices. Thus, in apparent contradiction to (or ignorance of) their own theology, they cannot accept God's forgiveness. Instead, they continue to live in a state in which their head knowledge and heart knowledge do not match. Like the servant in the parable, they have been told of the Lord's forgiveness, but their guilty emotions still demand retribution and repayment.

Intimacy restored

Restoring intimacy is the second aspect of forgiveness, and it is perhaps best understood in the
parent–child relationship. When a child chooses
to do something wrong, what does a healthy, loving parent need to see happen? The parent
needs to know that the child takes full responsibility for her choice and that she demonstrates a
genuine sorrow for her actions—not merely dis-
pleasure over being caught or suffering the consequences. If acceptance of responsibility and
appropriate sorrow are in place, the path to reconciliation and restored intimacy is completely cleared.
If not, can the relationship between parent and
child continue on a close and honest level? Of
course not.

And what if, at the point of the child's genuine repentance, the parent responds with cold detachment or harsh, sarcastic remarks? What if the
parent withholds love and forgiveness until a long
period of "good behavior" is established? Is this
the response of a loving parent? Unfortunately,
this is the response of parents all too often, especially when they are angry, weary, and frustrated.
Because we tend to form our concepts of God
during childhood, based upon the behavior of
our own parents, many people develop a distorted idea of the way God operates.[2]

One of the most touching illustrations of
God's forgiveness is found in the parable of the
prodigal son in the New Testament (Luke 15).
After leaving home with his inheritance and

squandering it on wine, women, and song, the son eventually finds himself starving in a pigpen. As he begins to remember the benevolence of his father's household, and the kindness his father showed to even the lowliest of servants, he comes to his senses and repents of the terrible decisions he has made. Knowing that he doesn't deserve to be received back as a son, he formulates a plan to return to his father and beg to be hired as a servant. After all, the lifestyle of even the servants in his father's house is better than what he is currently experiencing.

Meanwhile, the father has been at the gate every day since his son left, hoping and praying that he will return. And now, suddenly, a weary figure trudges toward the estate. In great joy the father receives him, sparing no expense with the "welcome home" party and lavishing him with expensive gifts. Interrupting the son's prepared speech requesting a place among the servants, the father bursts out with great emotion, "Nonsense! You are my son, and I am overjoyed to have you home!"

Like the son in this parable, many post-abortion women just want to "go back home," longing for the days before all the pain started. They've written off the possibility of enjoying a close relationship with God but would be happy just to be "in the fold." I have heard women actually verbalize that they would be content if they could be allowed to pitch their tent somewhere out in the boondocks of God's kingdom, like a foot soldier who is unknown to the general but still part of the army.

Punishment and consequences

The third aspect of forgiveness has to do with understanding the difference between punishment and consequences, which are all too easily confused. In the story of the prodigal son, there was no punishment given by the father, but he could not magically create a new endowment for his son. Although the relationship was completely restored, the son had to live for the rest of his life knowing that he had wasted his inheritance. The father could soften that blow somewhat by providing for him, but the squandered fortune was gone.

Sometimes we make decisions that result in consequences we would like to reverse, but we are powerless to do so. For the post-abortion woman one such consequence might be infertility. In the midst of that emotionally charged situation she might be tempted to interpret her inability to become pregnant as a sign of God's continued judgment and rejection. Instead, she needs to understand God's care for her and his limitless capacity to redeem the fallout from unwise choices in a fallen world.

I am reminded of the time our daughter Carrie, then seven years old, took our extremely tame but dim-witted cockatiel out of his cage in the backyard. She believed that he would be content to perch on her hand, as he always had done in the confines of the house. But when this bird felt the sunshine on his shoulders, he was history! He soared on unclipped wings to the freedom of the skies and was never seen again.

Was Carrie absolutely and genuinely sorry for taking the bird out of the cage? Absolutely. She fully understood the foolishness of her action. She was brokenhearted, and her remorse continued for months after the incident. As sad as I felt for Carrie, there was utterly nothing I could do to bring that bird back (although, for her sake, I would have paid good money to see him return). Carrie begged forgiveness for letting him out, and the family forgave her completely, but she had to live with the painful consequences of that action for a very long time.

God, as a loving parent, is as grieved as we are about the losses brought on by our choices and our remorseful longing to go back in time in order to make different decisions. In fact, knowing what lies ahead, he is no doubt saddened well before we are. But living with the consequences of our choices is an integral part of the uncoerced relationship God desires to have with us. If he were to step in and repeatedly override the adverse consequences of the choices we make, there could be no real free will and no real power to choose. Our choices would be meaningless because any decision we made would automatically be fixed by an indulgent and paternalistic Father.

One of the most poignant expressions of loss, grief, and repentance was penned by King David. In order to possess a beautiful woman, he had her husband killed in battle and later suffered the loss of their first child. In great pain, he came to God broken in spirit and without rationalizations for his actions:

> Have mercy on me, O God, because of your
> unfailing love.
> Because of your great compassion, blot out
> the stain of my sins.
> Wash me clean from my guilt. Purify me
> from my sin.
> For I recognize my shameful deeds—they
> haunt me day and night. . . .
> Purify me from my sins, and I will be clean;
> Wash me, and I will be whiter than snow.
> Oh, give me back my joy again; you have
> broken me—now let me rejoice.
> Don't keep looking at my sins. Remove the
> stain of my guilt.
> Create in me a clean heart, O God. Renew
> a right spirit within me.
> —from Psalm 51

And God restored David and forgave him.

Obstacles to Receiving Forgiveness

Many women have great difficulty accepting forgiveness. I have observed several reasons for this.

Poor relationship with a human father

Trusting fully in God is a frightening proposition for someone who has never experienced a healthy, trusting relationship with an earthly father. The Bible repeatedly identifies God as our "heavenly Father," and a woman's capacity to see God as nurturing and approachable will be greatly influenced by her interactions with her father (or whoever has filled that role in her life) during childhood, adolescence, and even adulthood.

Reluctance to give up "victimhood status"

Holding on to one's "defectiveness" can become an excuse for failing to move forward as a new, whole, healthy person. Moving toward healing and wholeness may be frightening because it means giving up old ways of coping. When I was in my late twenties, I began a counseling process that was long overdue. After successfully working through the issues I was struggling with, and after many insights into my reactions to a variety of life situations, my therapist began moving me toward "graduation." As she continued to talk about bringing our sessions to an end, I started to panic. It took me awhile to figure out that I had thought of myself as defective and inadequate for so long that the thought of being considered "healed" was extremely uncomfortable. I was afraid that I could not meet the expectations of a new role as "Fully Functional and Responsible Adult."

Inability to relinquish the belief that she must suffer longer

Some post-abortion women who have become grief-stricken over their abortion decision(s) feel that it is actually unjust to accept a release from guilt based upon a simple, humble request to God. When a woman is stuck because of this issue, I challenge her to compare her resistant feelings to the teachings of her faith. If a woman intellectually believes the tenets of a faith that teaches God forgives, but she is having trouble experiencing this doctrine on an emotional level, I will ask her to recognize the inconsistency and then make a conscious decision to believe God has forgiven her.

History of early sexual abuse

The majority of post-abortion women whom I have counseled have experienced some form of early sexual abuse. Whether the abuser was her father, step-father, her mother's live-in boyfriend, or someone else, the impact on a woman's capacity to think of God as a loving, safe "heavenly father" is great. I am presently counseling with a married post-abortion woman who was molested on a regular basis from ages seven through thirteen by a brother who was eight years older. Because there was no father in the home, the mother relied heavily on this older brother to be "the man of the house." As is sadly true in so many early sexual abuse stories, Mom also chose to not believe her daughter about the abuse. Although she is a Christian who is active in her church, this woman's view of the character of God is toxic. Helping her separate her feelings about her older brother (father figure) from her feelings about God (her heavenly Father) will be a long process.

115

❖ ❖ ❖ ❖ ❖ ❖

I asked the women in our group what question was the hardest to answer in the journaling project.

Cassandra: The whole thing was fascinating for me. Obviously, one of the main points is that our ideas about God come from our parents, especially our father. My dad was an alcoholic, and he was a mean drunk! If my ability to have a relationship with God is based on what I learned from him, I'm in trouble! My father was so random. He'd smack me around one night and give me $100 the next night because he'd sobered up and felt so guilty. After my brother and I were out of the house, my mom left him. He finally cleaned up his act—been sober for five years now. He's made his "amends" with me, along with all the other stuff AA tells them to do, but I'll never be close to him.

Thinking of "God the Father" makes me feel kind of wistful, rather than being a turn-off. It sounds so fairy tail-ish, but what if there really is a God out there who would be like the father I never had?

Cindy: For me the hardest questions were "Does it feel like God loves you?" and "Does it feel like God likes you?" I had a hard enough time with the first question because I know on an intellectual basis that God loves me but rarely feel it. When I came to the second question, I was just stunned. I had to answer that I did not feel that God "likes" me at all. Far from it! I feel like he probably can barely tolerate the thought of me, assuming that he ever actually thinks about me.

I'm so tired of feeling like no matter how hard I try, I'm never going to get back into God's favor again. But I can't stop trying. I have to make what I know in my head match up with my heart! I can't walk away from the church because I would be walking away from what I know to be true and right. But the difference between my head and my heart is killing me!

Jenny: Well, the part about describing the perfect parent is where I lost it. My grandfather molested me from age five through thirteen, and my parents didn't do a thing about it. I tried to tell them and they wouldn't listen.

How can I relate to a God who would allow that to happen to a little kid? If God loves me so much, why did he let all these bad things happen? My life has been a living hell since I was five years old. Most of the time I can numb myself and not think about God, but then something like this comes along and it gets stirred up all over again. I hate myself!

Shana: Jenny, I was molested, too, when I was a little girl. It was our next-door neighbor. His daughter was my best friend. He would wait and get me alone and then masturbate in front of me. I was terrified. I didn't do anything. It was like I was rooted to the floor while he would do this. When someone came near, he would stop and go into another room. To this day I can't believe I stood there—frozen like a deer caught in the headlights.

I tried to tell my mother but she wouldn't listen. I don't remember exactly what she said, but I know I felt very . . . dirty after I tried to talk to her about it, as if it was my fault or something. I never brought it up again, but he kept doing it for a long time.

I think that affected my spiritual search. I guess it was too painful to contemplate the existence of a God who could let terrible things happen to little kids who couldn't protect themselves, so I just decided to erase him from the universe. That sounds pretty arrogant when you say it out loud, huh?

Teri: I think so much of what we believe or don't believe about God is never verbalized or known to us on a conscious level. That's why I bring it into this healing process.

Chapter Six

Releasing the Anger

❖ ❖ ❖ ❖ ❖ ❖

One helpful post-abortion study is called *Forgiven and Set Free*.[1] The chapter on anger is particularly insightful. After working through that chapter, the women I met with had different responses to the topic.

Cindy: I got in touch with a *lot* of anger this week as I was doing the homework. And I have to tell you, it felt wonderful! It's like someone just gave me permission to "do" anger, and I'm shocked at how much was down there waiting for the green light. It's funny, but it doesn't really scare me to think of letting all that anger come to the surface. All my life I've been taught that anger is very, very, very bad and "good girls don't get angry." I have no idea why I've allowed myself to break past that barrier. It's not like me at all! But I found out I can tell myself that I'm not an angry person until I'm blue in the face, but inside I really *do* have a lot of anger about different things. If I don't deal with it, it's going to eat me alive.

Jenny: I've been angry all my life, it seems. So I didn't have *any* trouble getting into the homework. I'm angry at so many people I didn't know where to start. But still there's a huge part of me that's very resistant to starting this process. I feel like if I go to this place, I may never find my way back. I'm not convinced it's going to be worth the effort because I don't know if I'll be okay when I come out the other side.

Shana: I sort of feel like Jenny. There's something down there that's very toxic, and I'm not sure I want to give it a chance to speak. I asked myself, "Who are you really angry with?" and the answer was "Myself." I'm so angry at myself for having the abortion.

Cassandra: I found out that I'm very confused about my anger. I kept feeling like I was incredibly angry with Tom, which is completely crazy because he's such a great husband. I need help sorting that out because I didn't get very far with it on my own.

❖ ❖ ❖ ❖ ❖ ❖

Most women who seek counseling after an abortion have a tremendous amount of anger. Whether it is readily accessible or deeply suppressed often depends on how much time has elapsed since the abortion, as well as what they learned early in life about how to deal with negative feelings. If the abortion occurred within the past year or two, it is easier to recognize the anger. But as time passes without dealing with the negative feelings, these dark emotions will tend to become more suppressed.

Some women are not afraid of their anger. Most, however, resist identifying and expressing their negative emotions. I have heard women say in many different ways: "If I go to that bleak, unlit place inside me, I may get in touch with a rage that will lead to a total loss of control." And control is everything to someone who is trying to function in the wake of unresolved trauma.

Many people are raised in homes where it is not only considered wrong to express anger but *any* display of negative emotions is off-limits. If a woman grew up in a religious home she may be particularly hampered in this area because she has heard countless sermons exhorting her not to be angry.

For all of these reasons, a post-abortion woman often has difficulty deciding whether or not it is okay to talk about her anger. She may wonder *why* anger should be addressed as part of the healing process. At face value, digging up anger seems counterproductive to calming and healing emotions. But until the anger is identified, it lies beneath the surface like a pool of toxic waste threatening to boil up. The paradox is this: until the post-abortion woman is willing to stop denying the pain she felt (and still feels) about her abortion, she will never get rid of it.

If a woman's parents were involved in the abortion decision, she may have a particularly tough time dealing with anger toward them. This is especially true if that relationship has otherwise been decent during the years since the abortion. Most people feel it is disloyal to harbor ongoing hostility toward parents. They understand that their parents were trying to do what appeared to be the right thing at the time. But if feelings of betrayal still lurk below the surface, an intimate relationship between parents and grown child will be nearly impossible.

Forgiveness

A woman usually understands that if she deals with her anger she will have to forgive someone she doesn't want to forgive. This may cause her to further resist facing her anger. She may mistakenly believe that she has no options other than seething hostility or warm, fuzzy feelings. It may be helpful for her to think about *releasing the anger* rather than forgiving someone. We need to *let go* of the need for vengeance against the person(s) who wronged us. No glowing, positive feelings are required to accomplish this. Forgiveness is a decision rather than an emotion.

The purpose of dealing with the anger is not to have only a temporary experience of release. The goal is to unearth the destructive anger that has affected every important relationship since the abortion and to get rid of it *forever*. Recognizing and acknowledging the anger clears the path to genuine and permanent forgiveness.

It is important not only to admit that the anger is there but to decide *what kind* of anger is held. Some women cling to an anger in which everyone and everything is blamed for the abortion decision, allowing the woman to avoid any responsibility for it. There is a different, more useful kind of anger that says, "I can take responsibility for my choice, recognizing that those who should have been the most helpful to me actually participated in making a decision that hurt me." The difference is in the concept of *shared* blame. As long as a woman refuses to accept any responsibility for her abortion, she will remain the victim who is not able to direct the events of her life. When she acknowledges her role in the abortion decision, her peace and sense of wholeness no longer depend upon other people's choices. She has taken herself out of the victim role and now has the power to let go of the anger she feels toward others.

Sharing responsibility for the abortion allows the woman to forgive herself as well. A woman cannot forgive herself until she admits that there is something for which to be forgiven. Once she forgives herself, the path to forgiving others is cleared.

Identifying the Targets of Anger

An important part of facing anger and recognizing the need for forgiveness is to identify the targets of anger. For instance, a woman may be angry at the father of the aborted baby, a parent, a close friend, the abortionist, herself, or God. Sometimes her anger can be directed at someone who had nothing to do with the abortion at all— her husband or current boyfriend, for example.[2]

I will often have a woman make a list of the people who had anything to do with the abortion decision. Then I give her a piece of paper with a circle drawn in the middle. Using a pencil with an eraser, she divides the totality of her anger into portions, like pieces of a pie, assigning what she would consider to be a fair share to each person on her list. This becomes a visual picture to help her understand where her anger is directed. I then ask her to explain specifically why she is angry at each person.

Next I ask her to write each person on her list a letter that begins, "Dear _____: I am angry with you because. . . ." If she has put herself on the list, I have her write a letter to herself. Often a woman will be angry at someone not for pushing her to have an abortion but for taking the stance, "I'll support you in whatever you decide to do." Many women express deep resentment against a boyfriend or husband who thought he was doing the modern thing by letting the decision be hers alone. Instead, she desperately wanted him to say, "This is our baby. We'll make this work somehow." She feels that he should have been strong when she was most vulnerable. Her hostility may run deep for years after that time.

These letters—which are a journaling exercise and are never sent—may be a woman's first opportunity to verbalize long-held pain and anger. Often as a woman writes each person a letter she discovers that her anger toward some people was misdirected. She may also realize that there are others who deserve a larger piece of the "pie."

Reading the letter aloud often helps focus

anger more accurately. A woman frequently changes the portions she has assigned after discussing her drawing with someone else or after hearing about other women's drawings within a support group. She may realize that someone on her list doesn't actually merit a piece of the anger or that someone who wasn't originally on the list needs to be added. If someone has neglected to give herself a piece of the pie or if she has given herself a huge piece, I will ask her to explain her choice.

This is an example of how one woman's "pie" might appear:

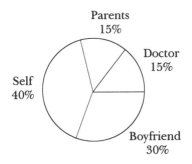

Sometimes a woman can easily extend compassion toward another post-abortion woman but she cannot forgive herself. If used in a group setting, this exercise can point out the inconsistency between a woman's standard for someone else and the harsher standard she applies to herself.

Should I Try to Make Amends?

After a woman has successfully released her anger

125

toward someone involved in the abortion episode, she often asks, "Should I try to talk with that person?" There is no easy answer to this question. Before seeking reconciliation with an individual, it is helpful to consider four questions:

◆ What is my motivation for communicating with this person?
◆ What do I think might be gained?
◆ Am I likely to get what I am seeking from this person?
◆ How will it affect me if I *don't* get what I need from this person?

When these questions are answered honestly, it usually becomes apparent whether or not a conversation with the individual is a good idea. For instance, if there has been no contact with the father of the aborted baby for a decade, he might not care one way or another. An attempt at reconciliation would be futile at best and could cause more distress. On the other hand, if the father of the baby is someone with whom the woman has contact and there has been a silent pain in the relationship since the abortion, then it could be beneficial to both people to talk about it.

Sometimes a woman had an abortion against the wishes of a husband, boyfriend, or parent. After finding forgiveness for herself, she desires to ask forgiveness for excluding the other person from the abortion decision. Before doing so, the same four questions need to be answered. It is painful indeed to seek absolution from someone who is not likely to offer it. (This topic is further addressed in the section "Deciding Whom to Tell" in chapter 8.)

Blocks to Releasing the Anger

A woman who is having trouble working through her anger may not have dealt with her personal guilt. It may be helpful for her to think about what purpose her anger serves. Perhaps it is frightening for her to no longer have someone to blame. She may be afraid that healing would be disloyal to her aborted child. Perhaps feeling ugly and angry toward herself and others is part of her "penance." Something inside her needs to hold on to that damaged self-concept. If the woman holds a Judeo-Christian worldview, it may be helpful for her to think about, "If God has forgiven me, what basis do I now have for withholding forgiveness from myself? And if I have forgiven myself, what basis do I now have for withholding forgiveness from anyone else?"

One exercise I use with women who are struggling to release anger is to ask them to reverse roles with whoever is the target of her anger. This means asking her to pretend she is that person, while I "play her" in dialogue. Sometimes, as the woman speaks for the other person, she begins to understand that the other person was motivated by wanting what he or she thought was the best thing for her at the time. If she can come to a place of believing that the other person was at least *trying* to help (however misguided they may have been), she may begin to release her anger toward that person and even, with time, forgive them.

Long-held anger becomes a habit and making the decision to live without it is not always an overnight process. But in the final analysis, releasing anger is just that—a decision.

❖ ❖ ❖ ❖ ❖ ❖

After the journaling exercise of writing letters to the people on their "pie" list, the women in our group had further thoughts about anger and forgiveness.

Jenny: Of all the people I'm angry at, my mom is at the top of the list, way out ahead of whoever is in second place. Writing her letter was *extremely* therapeutic for me! You have no idea how furious I've become at my mom since starting this group. She made me have an abortion when I was five months pregnant! I was fourteen years old. She wouldn't even stay in the room with me. I was in labor and had to deliver a dead fetus into a bedpan by myself. I don't know if I can ever forgive her for abandoning me then. I hate her. I blame her for everything. She looked the other way when my grandfather molested me. I blame her for the drugs I took to numb the pain. I blame her for the lousy husbands I chose. I blame her for my whole miserable life.

I don't know what it would be like to live without anger. I've lived with it for so long I don't know how to put it down at this point. It is who I've become. No wonder my husband left last April. I wouldn't want to live with me either.

Teri: Jenny, you have no control over your mother's actions, past or present, right? All you have control over is you. *You* control your choices and your behavior now. No one else. My sense is that you had so little control when you were a little girl that you never figured out that somewhere along the line you became an adult who had the power to make her own choices. So you keep operating as if you were still a powerless child. You put up this tough exterior, but really you're still a frightened little girl who doesn't know how to keep bad things from happening to her, who is bewildered and angry when bad things happen to her, who still can't figure out why she's been abandoned by the people who were supposed to love her.

Jenny: I don't want to be a little girl anymore. . . . Someone else go. That's all I can take for one night.

Shana: How about I tell you how my letter-writing went? I wrote two anger letters. One to myself and one to my trusted ob/gyn. I'm actually thinking about sending his for real! I wrote to that horrible doctor first. He should have his licensed revoked for making me feel like I had to have the abortion so quickly. He knew John was adamantly opposed to it, but he just plunged ahead and convinced me that I had to do it and do it *fast.* He told me I was at a very high risk for having a Down syndrome baby at my age. I found out later that the risk for that had only gone up a few percent or something.

None of my other children knew I was pregnant. It was bad enough dealing with John. But I was sitting here and realizing that the only person I should really be angry at is myself. I mean, a huge part of me wants to blame the doctor, and no one else, for the decision. But I'm not exactly a shrinking violet. I made the decision, and I cut John out of the loop. The bottom line is that I didn't want a newborn at age forty-one. And I've never really admitted that before tonight. I hate hearing myself say that. It makes me feel very ugly and very selfish. I lost my fifth child, I may lose my husband, and I have no one to blame but myself. It's not like I can go back and undo the abortion. I've tried apologizing to John, but there's a gulf between us now that I can't seem to repair.

Cindy: I'm kind of the opposite from you, Shana, as far as husbands go. I realized this week how angry I am at Bill. His family doesn't know we had the abortion. They don't even think we were having sex before we were married. They'd absolutely freak if they knew! My mother-in-law is "Mrs. Pro-Life" at her church. Sometimes at family dinners I have to sit there and listen to her talk about "those women who kill their children." I just want to crawl under the table and die when she gets started. Bill won't talk about it. He was very hostile about me doing this group. He is so scared his family is going to find out. We've been married eight years with no children, even though we've been seriously trying for the last three. I really don't know if we're going to make it.

Cassandra: At least your husband knows you're here. I think I'm about ready to confront Tom and tell him the truth. I'm tired of feeling like the defective one in our marriage. I'm tired of feeling like I have to apologize for taking up precious space on this planet. I'm so very, very tired.

Between doing the homework and listening to everyone tonight, something has snapped in me. I can't spend the rest of my life like this. I *won't* spend the rest of my life like this. I married Tom because he was such a good man and something in me knew I needed that. But it's backfired somehow. Instead of drawing me into his "goodness" I only feel more and more defective by comparison. I haven't told him about the abortions because . . . I'm afraid he would stop loving me. And I hate him for that! So I just keep wearing this mask and he doesn't really know me. But I can't wear the mask anymore. I just want to be me. I want to be loved for who I am, abortions and all. I want my husband to accept me as I am. I love him so much but I feel so angry at him because he only loves the Cassandra I've constructed for him!

Teri: Have you ever given him the chance to prove otherwise? Have you ever tested your theory by letting him see the less-than-perfect Cassandra and seeing what he does with it?

Cassandra: No. I've been afraid to find out. I could lose him. But I can't keep the facade going anymore. I'm going to tell him. I have to.

Chapter Seven

Accepting the Loss

❖ ❖ ❖ ❖ ❖ ❖

I asked the women in the group how they were feeling about approaching the topic of grief.

Cindy: I don't know if I would have been able to sign on if I had known in the beginning that we were going to do this. But I guess it's going to be okay.

Shana: I'm really having a problem with this whole thing—so what's new? I'm having a hard time getting it. Not only was I the one who chose to have the abortion, I did it against John's express wishes. Now I'm supposed to feel sorry for myself and go through a grieving process? This is nuts! Sure I've wondered if it was a boy or a girl and things like that. Sometimes I'm sure it was a girl because I have all boys. For a year after the abortion I found myself looking at little girls and wondering what it would have been like to buy frilly things for a change. Decorating her room, stuff like that.

Cindy: Me too—I've decorated that nursery a hundred times in my head!

Jenny: I'm feeling a little confused. I found myself this week thinking a lot about the first baby, but not the other two. So I feel guilty. I mean, shouldn't I feel as bad about the other two?

Teri: Not necessarily. Your first one was very different from the others. You were five months pregnant and you had a saline abortion so you actually saw the baby. And you felt terribly abandoned by your mom.

Jenny: Abandoned by my mom. Just like I abandoned my babies. . . .

Cassandra: I have the same situation. The first one bothers me so much and the second one is such a blur. I think it has everything to do with the fact that Sam was the first guy I ever loved, and he left me when I most needed him. I won't ever forget that feeling. But I want to tell you guys something that happened. I told Tom about the abortions this week. I found out that I married the guy I had *hoped* I married! He was incredible. We talked for about two hours straight one night after I had put Laurel to bed. The bottom line is that I did *not* get the judgmental reaction from him that I was so afraid of. That *proves* there's a God, right? Anyway, he said that it explained a lot to him, that I had given him the missing pieces he needed. He couldn't have had a better reaction than if I'd given him the script! And I am so sick that I have kept this secret from him for three years. That was the part that wounded him—remember at the first session, I told you I was afraid that would hurt him more than the actual abortions?

I finally get the chance to be the real me. And I couldn't believe it, but Tom brought it up again last night and told me he wants to adopt my aborted children. He wants to mourn with me as if they were his children, too. I am overwhelmed by his reaction, but I am so angry at myself for what I could have had with him for the past three years.

Teri: We'll be talking about losses during these next couple of sessions. We're specifically focusing in on the loss of your babies, but all kinds of other losses will come up as well. It is almost impossible to think of one loss without thinking about all the loss in your life.

❖ ❖ ❖ ❖ ❖ ❖

Why should a woman who is already hurting after an abortion deliberately contemplate the pain of losing that child? She has already dealt with many negative emotions. Doesn't it almost seem cruel for her to face the crushing reality of acknowledging her pregnancy loss?

When a woman becomes pregnant, she instinctively knows her life has changed forever. The bonding process between mother and child begins very soon after an initial period of dazed and conflicting emotions. If the pregnancy was unplanned, the woman will go through a short period of ambivalent feelings: euphoria alternating with dismay, the wonder of creating a new life squaring off against the pressures of the current circumstances. But even as a woman wrestles with the clash of feelings, a bond is being forged that is arguably stronger than any other bond. When that bond is broken—even when it is the mother's choice to break it—something is ripped out of the woman's soul.

The ache for the aborted child is described well in actress Ally Sheedy's poem "Local Anesthesia":

> I wish I could shake him off me . . .
> I know how hard he clutched me from the inside when they took him out.
> Now he dances bodiless tapping round my head like rain.
> When it was over I lay so still they thought I was in shock.
> But I was only saying good-bye to him.
> And you never can.
> 'Cause, child, I hear you in my head and on you cry like rain
> and I can feel you at my heart;
> inside I nurse you still.[1]

Anyone who has ever lost a baby knows how comments from others can be woefully inadequate: "Well, aren't you glad you miscarried early on instead of later?" "You should feel lucky. Miscarriage is just the body's way of rejecting a defective fetus." "Good thing you're young—you've got lots of time to have as many children as you want." The person who has never lost a pregnancy cannot begin to understand that a woman who has lost a baby in any way has had a permanent hole ripped in her heart.

Awareness of the need to grieve the loss of an *aborted* child is almost nonexistent in our culture. It is thus very common for post-abortion women to approach the grieving process with trepidation and confusion. "How do I grieve the death of a child when I was the executioner?" they ask. They do not feel they have any right to a normal grieving process. But they also harbor mixed emotions because they *do* grieve for the lost child.

Seeing the Baby as a Real Individual

When we have lost a loved one, we summon our memories of that person to help process the loss. Old photo albums, favorite possessions, special gifts, and most of all the experiences that we hold in our hearts all become highly treasured. But a woman who has aborted a baby has none of these things. If she was awake for the procedure, her only memories may be disturbing or even horrifying: the sound of material (which she may later realize were body parts) passing through a suction tube, or the sight of a lifeless body expelled hours after saline was injected into her uterus.

Therefore, the first component of grieving is for the woman to understand that she aborted a real, human baby. It may help for her to construct a picture of her child in any number of ways. She might imagine what sex she would have liked her baby to have been and describe what he or she might have looked like.

If a woman had an abortion several years ago, she will sometimes "see" her child as now being that number of years old. It is more common for a woman to visualize her aborted child as a small baby, perhaps because that seems a logical place to begin reconstructing their relationship. Either approach will work in the healing process.

Naming the child is also an important task because it gives the child a unique identity. Often a woman comes up with a name for the child easily, as if she thought about it subconsciously for a long time. A woman who may not have a clear picture as to whether it was a boy or a girl might choose an androgynous name such as "Jamie" or "Casey."

I sometimes ask a post-abortion woman to create an "album" for her child. Clipping images from magazines, she pastes pictures of mothers and children, various words, flowers, and so forth on the pages. These are chosen to represent her feelings about the relationship she wishes she could have had with her child. Parenting and baby magazines usually provide an ample supply of photos. *Victoria* magazines are especially popular because they are filled with soft and nostalgic pictures. I also make available stickers, stamps, and other pretty art supplies. If this exercise is done in the context of a group, we will take the first part of the session to work on the album and the second part for each person to talk through her album, explaining why she chose the items that were included. This album becomes an important part of her "memories" during the grieving process for her child.

Writing out feelings for the child

With an image of her child now indelibly etched

on her heart, she can proceed to the next phase of this task, which is giving herself permission to verbalize the sadness, regret, and longing of her loss. Additionally, this is an opportunity to ask the child's forgiveness and to declare her desire to one day be reunited (assuming she believes she will meet the child in an afterlife). This can be a very frightening experience for the woman who pictures her child now standing next to God, stretching an accusing finger down toward earth. This picture, of course, reflects her feelings of alienation from God. With healing, a woman will realize that nobody in God's presence could reflect anything but his love, compassion, and forgiveness.

A wonderful journaling project that can help a woman verbalize her feelings is writing a letter to her aborted child. Here, she can pour out her heart and explain (without excusing) her decision and the circumstances under which the abortion was obtained. She might tell the child how much he or she is missed, how sorry she is, how she longs to be reunited someday, and so forth. Here is an edited version of an actual letter:

> Dearest Baby:
> I don't know how to begin to write this letter. I am so ashamed that a big part of me feels I have no right to tell you my feelings. But I want you to know how sorry I am that I made the decision to abort you five years ago. I think about you so often. When I see a little girl your age, I never fail to think about you. Sometimes I cry when I think of

the experiences we have missed out on together. How I would have loved to plan your fifth birthday party with you this year. I dream about how you might have wanted it to be.

My child, I was so selfish five years ago. My heart aches to think that you paid the price for the terrible circumstances that I was surrounded with back then. I wish I had known then what I know now—that I really am a lot stronger than I thought. I could have had you and we could have made it work together. I'm so very sorry.

I hope, with all my heart, my love, that you are safe and happy now. You must be because you are with God. For a long time I couldn't think about being with you someday because I've been so ashamed of not letting you be born. But recently I've come to believe that you must be in a place where everything is made clear, so I'm asking you to forgive me. I hope someday we can see each other face to face. I finally believe this is possible. I will never forget you, my child.

Love, Your Mom

The purpose of writing the letter is *not* to attempt to communicate with her dead child in any way. Rather, it is to help a woman express her feelings about a real child—a necessary part of the grieving process. In addition, this exercise helps a woman gain a clear understanding of where she believes her child is and what their relationship will be when they are reunited. The goal is for her to complete her grieving process with the assurance that reconciliation *will* happen when she sees her child someday.

Where is the baby now?

Most women I counsel, whether or not they have a well-defined spiritual creed, verbalize the belief that their aborted baby must be with God, or that their baby exists somewhere and has self-awareness.

Most women have been raised with an understanding that young infants who die prematurely go directly to be with God. Those who are familiar with the Bible may cite King David's words after the death of his and Bathsheba's son. Once he learns of the infant's death, David takes off his mourning clothes. His advisors are confused. "We don't understand you. While the baby was still living you wept and refused to eat. But now that the baby is dead, you have stopped your mourning and are eating again." To this King David replies: "I fasted and wept while the child was alive. . . . But why should I fast when he is dead? Can I bring him back again? I will go to him one day, but he cannot return to me" (2 Samuel 12:21-22).

The concept that there is an "age of accountability" before which children are deemed innocent by God is derived from two Old Testament Scriptures. Isaiah 7:15 states, "By the time this child is old enough to eat curds and honey, he will know enough to choose what is right and reject what is wrong." And in Deuteronomy God declares to the disobedient wandering children of Israel, "You will never enter the Promised Land. . . . I will give the land to your innocent children" (1:37,39). The psalms of the Old Testament contain several assurances that God has a special heart for unprotected children, including, "Even if my father and mother abandon me, the LORD will hold me close" (Psalm 27:10).

When working with a Catholic woman, I make sure she has a copy of Pope John Paul II's *Message to Post-Abortion Women:*

> I would like to say a special word to women who have had an abortion: The Father of mercies is ready to give you his forgiveness and his peace in the Sacrament of Reconciliation. You will come to understand that nothing is definitely lost and you will also be able to ask forgiveness from your child, who is now living in the Lord (Evangelium Vitae— The Gospel of Life, Paragraph 99).

If a woman is firm in her resolve that her child is not with God, I do not try initially to dissuade her from this belief. Rather, I simply encourage her to reflect on what she has learned so far about the compassionate nature of God and then to consider how she believes a tender God would deal with her innocent child.

The Memorial Service

A memorial service for a loved one who has died

is perhaps the most enduring of all human rites. Commemorating the loved one's life and passing is an important part of the grieving process. This is especially true for the woman who has lost a child before birth because there is so little evidence that her child ever existed. I am always impressed at the sense of peaceful closure the memorial service brings to the end of counseling or support groups. This sense of closure does not mean that a woman will never again grieve for the child. In the next chapter I discuss how the post-abortion woman can handle future periods of remembrance and mourning.

Most women recognize the memorial service as a necessary step in the healing process. Not only is this a time of acknowledging the death of her child but it is also a milestone of her healing to this point. It provides hope for her future, confirming that she has at last worked through this very painful episode in her life, and reinforcing her belief that she is the recipient of God's good will.

The woman should design the service so that it feels extremely personal and will meet her particular needs. Usually it is a very simple affair. At its minimum, a memorial service might include a solemn time set aside at the end of a group session (approximately fifteen minutes for an individual; half hour to one hour for a group). A meaningful song is played during this time of silence, after which the woman is encouraged to say a few words about her healing process and her feelings about her child. A concrete memento of this special time is given to keep with the other things she has accumulated during previous sessions (such as the memory book, the letter she wrote). I try to be creative with this keepsake, making it unique for each woman. For instance, if she had two abortions, I might buy a tiny double heart frame and put the children's names in the frames. We end with perhaps another song, a prayer, and many warm hugs.

Some women have chosen to conduct a much more involved observance. Since this may involve a potential violation of confidentiality, it has to be completely comfortable for every member. Spouses, parents and/or friends—those who are closest to the woman and whom she wants to be there for support—are invited to this more traditional memorial service. Many local cemeteries have created a special area for memorial services. The service could take place in a local place of worship or a home. A woman might even invite a pastor, priest, or rabbi to conduct the service.[2]

Remembering that the women need to design the ceremony, the components of this more elaborate time of commemoration might include the following:

1. *Gathering:* Soft, reflective music is playing as participants arrive and continues to play during the commemoration part of the ceremony. If the service is conducted in a large area, dim the lights in the areas not being used (to promote intimacy). A printed

program with songs, order of service, and names of the children being commemorated is a nice keepsake.

2. *Introduction:* The clergy member or designated person reads Scripture and/or a poem selected by the women and acknowledges the purpose and significance of the memorial service.

3. *Commemoration:* Each woman comes forward and takes a symbol of remembrance (e.g., a rose) and speaks for a few moments about the child she is commemorating. For instance: This is to remember the life and death of my precious Joshua, whom I aborted and whom I dearly desire to see one day. She might then light a candle for her child(ren).

4. *Pastoral remarks:* The pastoral remarks should be extremely brief, recognizing the healing that has occurred during the group's time together. The pastor (or rabbi or priest) might individually bless each woman, giving her a brief personal encouragement and acknowledging God's complete forgiveness of her.

5. *Communion:* If a woman desires, the sacrament of Communion could be included.

6. *Closure:* Closing remarks, a special song if desired, and prayer.

7. *Refreshments:* An opportunity to share with each other afterward over light refreshments is important, helping the participants transition from a deeply emotional

time of sharing to resuming the normal activities of their lives.

Obstacles to Healing

If a post-abortion woman hasn't successfully worked through the prior steps of the healing process, it may be very difficult for her to find closure. Because not everyone follows a predictable path toward healing, it is not unusual for me to end a group with at least one woman still grappling with unresolved issues. She can be reassured that her feelings are common.

Sometimes a woman believes the false premise: "If I stay depressed long enough I can atone for my abortion by showing God, and my baby, and the world at large how very, very sorry I am." She may also believe that it is disloyal to the aborted child to allow herself to be happy and move on with her life and find enjoyment in her other children. (Anyone who has suffered the death of someone close will remember the guilt that arises on the inevitable day when the loved one has not been thought about for several hours.) This can become an unhealthy (or even obsessive) way of proving her love for the aborted child. Recognizing and understanding that those thoughts are untrue is an important step toward healing.

❖ ❖ ❖ ❖ ❖ ❖

The four women in our group were in different stages of the grieving process:

Cassandra: I feel like I can finally grieve for my babies. Tom's reaction has been so healing for me. I can't even begin to describe it. It's like I've gotten a whole new chance at life, you know? I'm ready to do this now.

Cindy: I'd give anything to have Bill's support. I'm so jealous of Cassandra. I wouldn't want to take away what you've experienced with Tom, and I'm so happy for you—I am. But it hurts. If anything, Bill has become angrier about me coming here. On one hand, I understand that he's threatened because I'm dealing with something he can't handle yet. But on the other hand, it feels as if he doesn't love me enough just to bear with me on this. I'd really like to have closure here, and I'm not sure I can do it without Bill. I've never felt more separated from him.

Teri: Cindy, would you try something with me? I want you to be Bill; try to imagine what his feelings are and speak for him as you think he would speak if he were being as honest as he could. Okay?

Cindy: Sure. . . . I'll try.

Teri: Bill, Cindy is so sad. She says you two have become really distant since she decided to attend the post-abortion support group.

Cindy (as Bill): Yeah. I don't understand why she wants to stir all this stuff up. It happened such a long time ago. We were young and scared, and we did something we shouldn't have done. But we can't go back and change history.

Teri: It must be very difficult for you to see her hurting and not to be able to help her.

Cindy (as Bill): I . . . [Cindy stopped and looked stunned.] It *is* hard to watch. I can't do anything to help her because I can't go back and change what we did.

Teri: What stops you from just listening to her and comforting her pain?

Cindy (as Bill): Because if I do that, I'll have to agree with her that what we did was wrong, and I'm not ready to look at that yet.

Teri: So what's it like to have Cindy on such a different page on this issue?

Cindy (as Bill): It hurts. This is the hardest place we've ever been. It hurts getting into bed every night feeling like your wife can't stand sleeping next to you. . . . [She hesitated and said something to herself.] Do I communicate that to him? Where did that come from?

Teri: Does Cindy blame you for not being able to get pregnant now?

Cindy: I *do* blame him. I never realized. I blame him for not stopping the abortion, for not going to his perfect Catholic family and admitting we were pregnant and making it all work somehow.

Teri: Cindy, what would happen if you went to Bill and told him you don't want to blame him anymore, that you just want to be able to mourn the loss of the child you conceived together?

Cindy: I don't know. I think he might respond to that. I didn't realize until tonight that he's probably been receiving a lot of anger from me. No wonder he hasn't given me the support I need so much. I don't know if I can do anything about it but I'm going to try.

Shana: I named my little girl this week. I knew you'd be shocked! The last of the cynics here actually dove head first and went for it! And I feel really, really good about it. I thought it would feel so stupid, but it doesn't. It feels complete. I wrote that letter and everything.

But I talked to John about all this. He was not exactly what you'd call supportive. He thinks I'm a world-class hypocrite for having the abortion and then turning around and wanting to name the baby. And since I'm still struggling with that myself, I can't really blame him. It feels okay to think about my baby and I really got into the homework, but I was dumb enough to talk to John about it, and then I felt a little foolish. Now that I'm here again tonight and listening to everyone, I know that it is *not* foolish. This week when I was talking to John about the homework, I actually *did* say something of an apology to him because I had the abortion even though he didn't want me to. He's not ready to hear it yet. I think I'm going to be paying for this one for a very, very long time.

Jenny: You said something last week that rang in my head all the way home. When we were talking about the way I saw the first baby, you said, You must have felt so abandoned by your mom. That really affected me. I cried myself to sleep that night. I was still thinking about it the next day. And you know what? All the anger I have had toward my mother all these years just melted away. I don't know exactly where it went, and I'm still not quite sure why it went away. Maybe because I was thinking, Well I abandoned my babies by aborting them, so how am I different from my own mother? I found myself feeling actual sorrow for her this week. Now *that's* a new feeling for me! Suddenly I just couldn't generate the old bitterness. Instead, I saw her as a broken woman, just doing the best she could with what she had—which wasn't much, given how *she* was raised. This all feels really different for me. But it only feels like a shaky beginning.

Chapter Eight

Moving On

❖ ❖ ❖ ❖ ❖ ❖

When a woman has experienced a profound healing in a post-abortion support group, she may be reluctant to move on without that group. The women in our group had much to say as we drew to a close.

Jenny: I think this group has been the most important thing that's happened in my life for a very, very long time, and I still don't even know how to describe why that is. I feel like something "monumental" has happened. But it's only starting. So I'm a little unsure about what comes next. The two most incredible shifts in my heart have been my willingness to look at God in a fresh light and my yearning to be reconciled with my mom. That's a lot coming from me! I can't exactly explain why, but all the old bitterness just isn't worth hanging on to anymore. I find I just want to find some peace in my life now, and let all that stuff slip away—all that stuff that was so important before.

Cindy: Exactly! I went home from last week's session and had a very long talk with Bill. Wow. I don't know whether to be excited about feeling so good about my husband again or completely depressed about the years we wasted not talking about it. It was as if the dam broke. It has been so hard for him—my coming to this group every week and working in my workbook in between. He felt so excluded and afraid I was moving on to a place that wouldn't include him. It helped me so much to put myself in his place. It was as though I had crawled into Bill's head just long enough to feel what he must be going through. And all the hurt I've had in the past few years on account of him just left.

I told him I wanted us to stop blaming each other and start being on each other's team again. He was so ready for that. It almost startled me how undefensive he was! We've been on cloud nine for the past few days. It's as if the past years have simply been erased. Oh, I know it's the "honeymoon" phase and that we still have a lot of stuff that needs to be talked about, but this feels so good!

Shana: I don't think I'm ready for this to be the last session. I don't exactly have "and they lived happily ever after" stamped on my life. Rather than being closer to my husband, I've never felt more distant from him. I feel as though I got so burned trying to approach him about this whole thing a couple of weeks ago. I'm not really interested in trying again. It feels as if the ball's in his court now, and I'm pretty sure it's going to stay there. Part of me wishes I had never started therapy because ignorance is bliss. But I think these feelings of alienation from John were always lurking in the background. It's probably better to know, I guess. Sure feels bad. On the brighter side, however, if I hadn't joined this group, I never would have learned that it's okay to think about my little girl and to miss her. That has been worth the other stuff for me.

Cassandra: I am so thankful I've been here. I've come to know who my husband is, who my aborted children are, and (most important) who *I* am. And I guess I'd have to add to the list that I've come to know who God is a little bit, too. I'd never really been to church before, but Tom and I decided to visit some different churches and find one we're comfortable in. We went to some kind of nondenominational Bible church in our neighborhood last Sunday. We liked it. This is a time of beginnings for both of us.

❖ ❖ ❖ ❖ ❖ ❖

Women have many reactions as their time of healing draws to a close. For some, the healing process has been long and arduous, though successful, and they are grateful to be at the end of this period of painful self-examination. Others may not have been able, for any number of reasons, to accomplish what they had hoped, and they may be feeling a bit lost and abandoned. At the end of a time of healing and counseling, it is crucial for a woman to identify the work that has been accomplished; to develop a plan for finishing the work that remains to be done; to decide who—if anyone—needs to be told about the abortion and subsequent healing process; and to prepare to handle the ongoing memories that will inevitably be a part of her life.

Identify the Work That Has Been Accomplished

A recovering woman needs to understand clearly where she is on the healing journey and how she plans to complete it. If she doesn't understand that her healing is an ongoing process, she will be repeatedly derailed by ongoing reminders and may even revert to an "I am eternally victimized" mentality. One effective means for assuring this sense of progress is to summarize what has happened so far. These questions will help her remember what she's learned:

Symptoms

- Has there been a substantial decrease in the symptoms that had previously paralyzed my daily routine?
- Have those closest to me seen an improvement in my mood and overall function?
- Has communication improved with those closest to me?
- (If married:) Do I now relate differently to my spouse?
- Do I feel more hopeful than when I started my healing work?
- Do I feel more whole than when I started my healing work?
- Do I feel confident that I can now address other issues in my life that need my attention?

Remembering

◆ Have I gained a clearer understanding of the events and feelings surrounding my abortion experience?

◆ Am I able to remember more details about my abortion now than when I started working through these struggles?

◆ Am I able to think about my abortion experience without disabling anxiety?

Guilt and forgiveness

◆ Have I accepted responsibility for my part in the abortion decision?

◆ Can I speak calmly about my abortion when it is appropriate to do so (but without feeling compelled to do so—especially publicly—as a form of "penance")?

◆ Do I "own" my abortion experience?

◆ Am I fearful of others finding out about my abortion? If so, who in particular? Is the list now the same as when I started?

◆ Do I accept God's forgiveness for my abortion?

◆ Does the exhilaration of understanding God's forgiveness, and forgiving myself, ultimately eclipse the fear of judgment from someone else?

◆ Do I feel that I deserve to move forward and lead a productive, rewarding life?

◆ Have I been able to turn off the mental "tapes" that have condemned me for so long?

Releasing the anger

◆ Have I released all who assisted and supported my abortion decision?

◆ Am I able to think about each of these individuals without bitterness?

◆ Am I still holding any grudges? Am I hoping that something bad will happen to someone who was involved with my abortion
decision?

◆ Do I understand that the others involved in
my abortion decision are solely responsible
for whatever burden of guilt they may feel
and that it is not my job to make them feel
guilty?

Grieving the loss

◆ Do I feel reconciled with my aborted
child(ren)?

◆ Am I looking forward to being reunited
someday with my child(ren)?

◆ Do I now feel that I can join in the celebra-
tion at the birth of someone else's child?

Developing a Plan for Finishing the Work That Remains to Be Done

The primary goal for a woman in recovery is to
reduce the number and intensity of the symptoms
she has been experiencing and to regain a sense
of control by understanding the impact of the
abortion in her life. It is completely unrealistic to

expect that someone who has experienced a deeply felt loss will never again grieve. Successful counseling and personal effort in dealing with post-abortion loss does not lead to a point where a woman never feels sorrow again. Instead, the goal is to help her learn that she is a whole person who can cope with the ongoing reminders when they arise, rather than becoming panic-stricken and immobilized.

Prior to her initial healing experience, a woman's post-abortion issues are like an accumulation of scraps of paper containing dirty little secrets that she has been stuffing into the pigeon-holes of an old-fashioned roll-top desk. Whenever an ugly wad (painful memory) appears on the desktop, she quickly crams it into one of the slots without actually looking at it, giving the false appearance that her desk is completely clean. But when she reaches that point in her life when her methods of coping are no longer working and she can no longer deny the pain, the resulting chaos is like the aftermath of a major earthquake. All the garbage that she has so diligently hidden for years now comes crashing down onto the work area of her desk (her day-to-day living experience).

As she works through her post-abortion pain, a woman engages in an intense "clean-out" during which she intentionally examines, classifies, and deals with all the garbage. Some she throws away (feelings of anger or unforgiveness, for example), while others, such as grief for the lost child, cannot be thrown away. These are carefully smoothed out and tenderly filed back into the proper pigeon-hole. The work area is organized. But inevitably, the original earthquake will send out "aftershocks": ongoing reminders that rumble through and send scraps of paper cascading down again onto the work area. Most are items that have already been classified and can be refiled without much work. A small percentage may be new scraps that remained hidden during the initial cleaning and were never dealt with. These may require a little more time to study and classify, file, or toss out. But no aftershock will cause the same amount of disruption to the work area as the first earthquake because the major cleanup effort has been already done. As other (previously undiscovered) scraps of paper fall onto the work space, she knows how to deal with them without allowing them to cause a major disruption in her life.

For many women, the work they have done will open the door to related issues that they now have the courage to face. For some a key is addressing early sexual abuse and understanding how it drastically affects her self-concept and her relationships with men. Others may experience a spiritual awakening that they will seek to nurture in a church or small group setting.

Some women will build relationships with other post-abortion women, perhaps those from a therapy group. (It is not unusual for long-lasting friendships to develop from these groups). Others may seek formal counseling on an individual basis.

Deciding Whom to Tell

When a woman has lived under the crushing shame of self-imposed silence about a past abortion, the sense of freedom that flows from her healing can be almost euphoric. She may feel an overwhelming urge to talk about her newfound liberty, but the implications of sharing her abortion experience with other people need to be carefully weighed. Before deciding to tell someone else about what has happened, she should think through the following questions:

1. What is my motive for telling this person?
2. What benefit will result from this person hearing what I have experienced?
3. What kind of response am I likely to receive from this person?

I encourage a post-abortion client or support group member to be very selective in her choice of people with whom she will talk about these experiences. Above all, I don't want a negative reaction to put her into a tailspin, and so I specifically prepare her for a possible range of responses. I also ask her to think through the potential impact of her revelation on the other person, and to consider carefully the appropriate time and place to broach this subject: not at the end of an evening when everyone is tired; not when children are crying, the dog barking and the phone ringing; not on Christmas morning or some other special occasion; not in the middle of an argument, a crisis, or a major upheaval; and most of all, not when there isn't time available to talk things over, assuming that the other person is willing to do so. This conversation cannot be a verbal bombing mission, where the woman drops her explosives and then flies away.

She needs to prepare her approach—writing it out like a script, if necessary—stating ahead of time what response she needs or would find most helpful if the other person can give it. Otherwise, he or she often may not know quite how to react, and the result could be an awkward, or even intensely painful, encounter. Here's an example of what she might say to the other person: "I'm going to tell you something about myself that I've never told you before. It's really hard for me to tell you this, and I'm really scared to do it. What I'm hoping you can give me in return, if possible, is your understanding and acceptance. I'm hoping that you won't judge or reject me. I don't need you to fix it. I've already worked through a healing process and I understand that you may need some more time to deal with this." Obviously her approach must be tailored to the particular person, their relationship, and the specific response the woman is seeking.

Young children. Generally speaking, a post-abortion woman's young children should not be told of her experience because they lack the intellectual and emotional capacity to understand their mother's abortion choice from an objective or compassionate viewpoint. Their feelings of

159

safety are likely going to be seriously threatened by the information that Mommy had the power to dispose of a baby. Sometimes school-aged children will ask a direct question out of the blue, such as "Mommy, was there a baby in our family before me?" I suggest that the woman answer a question such as this one as she might respond to a child's inquiry about sex: offer what he or she can understand and handle. An appropriate answer might be something like, "Mommy once had a baby growing inside her tummy who died before he could be born."

Teenagers. Adolescents are better equipped to handle this part of Mom's history if they are curious. Many parents worry about admitting that they made a "wrong turn" when they were young because they fear their teens will draw the wrong conclusion: "Well, *they* did it, so I can, too." Sadly, a pregnant teenager from a healthy family will often choose to have a secret abortion primarily because she believes her parents will be shocked, dismayed, and rejecting if they find out she has been sexually active. Sharing a past abortion decision with a teenage daughter can be done in a manner that says, "These are the choices I made and these are my regrets. But my desire is that you know that no one loves you as I do, and that even if you were to make the same mistake and become pregnant, I would never turn you away."

When an adolescent is told about the abortion, he or she needs to be given permission to be sad or angry for a while and to digest what took weeks to work through. In the majority of cases I have dealt with, the teenager before long will overcome these initial hard feelings and replace them with understanding.

It is also important to discuss confidentiality: "This is something I am entrusting to you. I will answer whatever questions you have, as often as you need to ask, but please do not share this with anyone else. I told you about this chapter in my life because I believe you are old enough to keep my confidence."

Parents. If a woman's parents (particularly her mom) never knew about the abortion, a decision to tell them now should be weighed very carefully. How many years has it been? How old are her parents? How well will they be able to handle the revelation? Will it serve to heal or improve the relationship?

If her parents were involved in procuring or even coercing the abortion, it is likely that there has been a great deal of unresolved guilt and that parents and daughter have not talked about it since, at least in any depth. In my experience, most parents who participated in an adolescent daughter's abortion—or who made that decision for her—honestly believed that it was in her best interest, were motivated by love and concern, and have long been dismayed at how profoundly their daughter was affected by their decision. If a post-abortion woman decides to approach her parents years later, the opportunity to air old feelings

161

and secrets can result in a sweet reconciliation. However, she also runs the risk of being rebuffed and must be prepared for this sad possibility.

If a woman is considering talking to a parent who helped her obtain the abortion, I might suggest that she say something like, "Please forgive me for having sex outside of marriage" (if this indeed was the parental value imparted to her as a teen). "I feel very bad about putting you in a position where you felt you had to help me get an abortion." This admission of the dilemma her parents faced tells them that she understands how they felt and how they believed they were doing the best thing for her at a time when she was not following the family's value system.

Spouse. Because a healthy marriage involves emotional intimacy, I usually—but not always—encourage a woman to tell her husband of her abortion history if she has never revealed it to him. Because this is (hopefully) her closest relationship, she needs to spend time carefully reviewing what she wants to say and how she might best present it to him. I follow up with everyone who is broaching this subject because it is such a risky thing to do, but I am especially careful with a woman who is about to tell her husband for the first time. If the marital relationship has deteriorated to the point that he is not likely to respond well to her, I need to help her process that rejection immediately.

If her spouse already knew about the abortion, it may now be appropriate to tell him how the healing process has changed her. If he was the father of the aborted child, this might provide an opportunity for him to experience some healing himself. On the other hand, he may be very threatened that she has been stirring these muddy waters. If he was not the father, he may have been hurt and confused that she has been in counseling or a support group to talk about issues arising from a sexual liaison with another man.[1] However, hopefully she can communicate with him not only the progress she has made but also how her healing is, and will continue to be, a benefit for their relationship.

Dealing with the Continuing Memories

My two brothers were killed in a plane crash on October 28, 1978. That was a long time ago. But for years after their deaths, I became ill and depressed as October 28 approached. I never made the connection that it was the anniversary of that very sad episode in my life. Once I finally understood that my body was remembering what I was trying to deny, I decided to start setting the day aside in order to take care of myself emotionally. While my need for this time-out has diminished over the years, the anniversary remains indelibly fixed in my brain.

As a post-abortion woman finishes therapy, she must be adequately prepared for the inevitable triggers—both environmental and personal—which might set off an emotional nose-dive, followed by some very panicky feelings: "Oh no . . . I did all that work for nothing!"

A woman must examine how she might feel on Mother's Day, Christmas, the anniversary date of her abortion, the next baby shower invitation, and so forth. She ought to think about those days and plan for them: How will I take care of myself on those days? What will I tell myself? How will I respond to the negative feelings that might come up on those days? Perhaps she needs to plan to take the day off and go to a quiet, private, safe place and journal her feelings. She may need to spend the day with a close friend who deeply understands the impact of her abortion and her subsequent healing process.

There is also a need to think through her response to stressful or transitional events in the future: marriage, the birth of a child, the loss of a family member, and so forth. What about unexpected, less dramatic, but still troublesome events that could occur in everyday life: TV shows in which the subject or plot line includes a crisis pregnancy or abortion; newspaper articles about the politics or personal impact of abortion; people who make insensitive remarks about women who have abortions? What about other crises that might occur unexpectedly, such as the loss of a job, divorce, sickness, and so forth? Will she interpret these events as a punishment from God or as a part of the natural order of things?

Obviously, it isn't possible for a woman to leave the healing process and never again grieve over her loss. She needs to know that it's okay to cry when fresh pain comes but that she will no longer be upended by feelings of panic or a suspicion that she is "going crazy." If she does not give herself permission to feel her grief occasionally, she will certainly begin to doubt her healing when such feelings arise unexpectedly. The goal is for her to understand that the abortion and its aftermath have been an important chapter in her life—but not the whole book—and that this chapter has essentially come to a close.

❖ ❖ ❖ ❖ ❖ ❖

Our group decided to meet for a "reunion potluck" six months after the memorial service. It was wonderful to see everyone together again.

Cassandra and Tom had become active in the little neighborhood church, and both had made professions of faith. She had just signed up to take a lay counseling course at a local crisis pregnancy center and was looking forward to serving as a volunteer. Needless to say, she looked remarkably different from the woman who had shown up at the first session of the post-abortion group. She displayed a self-confidence that was marvelous to watch. She and Tom had just celebrated their daughter's second birthday, and she talked about how much she was looking forward to becoming pregnant again. "I want to know what it's like to go through the whole thing without all the weirdness," she said. We understood exactly what she meant.

Cindy was finally pregnant and absolutely radiant. She happily showed off her first maternity top to the group and was showered with congratulations.

She and Bill had decided to begin some marriage counseling a couple of months after the group had ended, and she reported that this had been a time of hard but rewarding exploration for them. She and Cassandra had kept in touch after the group ended and were developing a good friendship. They were taking the lay counseling course together.

Shana and John had also started marriage counseling but, sadly, were separated at the time of our reunion. She was fighting depression and had just started individual counseling. "I have real mixed emotions about the group as I look back," she said. "A part of me would like to believe that my marriage never would have fallen apart if I hadn't attended, and if you hadn't made me be so honest with myself. But I know that this confrontation with John would have happened eventually. He cannot forgive me for having that abortion. He feels that it was the ultimate betrayal—of him, of our marriage, of God—and what can I say? I've said 'I'm sorry' so many different ways that I've lost count, and his unwillingness to forgive me is taking a real toll. I can't keep begging forever." The other three asked for her new number and offered to keep in touch. Shana gratefully accepted.

Jenny had gone to her mom as soon as the group ended and followed the script she had rehearsed. She told her mother how sorry she was for putting her in the position of having to deal with a fourteen-year-old daughter's crisis pregnancy. This approach softened her mother's heart, and she, in turn, tearfully confessed that she had for years felt incredibly guilty about coercing the abortion—but she hadn't known how to talk to her about it after so many years of accumulated pain. Jenny's mom was not yet willing, however, to listen to the story of the early sexual abuse by her grandfather. Jenny suspected that her mom had a similar tale carefully hidden in the dark recesses of her mind. She hadn't told her mom about the other two abortions yet. But she was content for now because she and her mom finally had been able to talk about the first abortion. It was, she hoped, the first of many steps in a healing journey for the two of them together.

I chose to write about Cassandra, Cindy, Shana, and Jenny for this book because their stories are so representative of the hundreds of women with whom I have worked. Like each of them, every woman has the opportunity to experience healing after an abortion. There is nothing more powerful than to receive a chance to "clean the slate," to feel pure and whole after a painful, shaming episode in one's life. My prayer in writing this book is that the reader will be left with true hope for peace after an abortion.

Appendix One

A Brief History of Post-Abortion Syndrome

❖ ❖ ❖ ❖ ❖ ❖

Prior to 1973, the majority of states either outlawed abortion or allowed it only in extreme situations: pregnancies arising from rape or incest, pregnancies threatening the life of the mother, or severe psychiatric illness. In 1973, however, the U.S. Supreme Court issued the historic 1973 *Roe v. Wade* decision that in one stroke removed virtually all legal barriers to abortion. During the first six months of pregnancy, abortion could be obtained on demand—no questions asked, other than the medical details necessary to conduct the procedure. During the final three months of pregnancy, abortion could be obtained to safeguard the health of the mother, with *health* defined in very broad terms, encompassing physical, emotional, and social well-being. Needless to say, this decision was one of the most important and controversial rulings ever handed down by the Supreme Court.

Individuals and groups supporting the *Roe v. Wade* decision argued that, without unrestricted access to abortion, millions of women with crisis pregnancies would suffer great emotional, and often physical, distress. They would be forced to carry and deliver babies they didn't want, often under profoundly adverse circumstances, or would be so desperate to end their pregnancies that they might subject themselves to the harrowing and dangerous world of the back-alley abortionist. *Roe v. Wade* supporters claimed that a legal abortion carried out by a well-trained physician in an office or clinic staffed by supportive counselors and nurses would be a humane solution to a wrenching problem and would ultimately help stabilize a woman's life.

Opponents to wholesale legalization of abortion stressed that this procedure victimized the innocent and defenseless unborn child, whose life was unjustly and violently terminated. The argument that legal abortion might have adverse consequences for the mother, on the other hand, was harder to sell. If pro-life advocates warned that an abortion could have significant medical complications, even when performed by a well-trained physician, their opponents quickly pointed out that (from a statistical standpoint) carrying a baby to term is actually more risky. They would also be sure to show horrific pictures of botched illegal procedures. Concerns about possible psychological effects of abortion were countered with the argument that few abortions, up to that point in time, had been carried out under safe and legal (let alone supportive) conditions. Any emotional impact from the procedure could thus be explained as the by-product of hostile circumstances. Even in states where abortion was legal, a woman typically had to run a humiliating gauntlet just to prove that she needed to end her pregnancy, let alone to have the procedure actually done. The possibility that abortion might cause emotional problems later in life seemed largely theoretical, often linked to concerns about moral guilt and spiritual well-being. In the culture of the late 1960s and early 1970s, when traditional values (especially regarding sexuality) were widely challenged or abandoned altogether, these lines of argument fell on increasingly deaf ears.

169

During the years immediately following the *Roe v. Wade* decision, the number of abortions performed in the United States swelled to more than 4,000 per day. Nevertheless, virtually no one in the popular press or professional publications raised any concern that post-abortion emotional problems might begin to appear on a widespread basis. It was naive, however, to believe that legalizing this procedure would somehow cause its psychological effects to vanish into thin air. Indeed, a 1981 poll commissioned by the Alan Guttmacher Institute (a research organization funded by Planned Parenthood) provided an insight into one of the important undercurrents of the abortion experience. Of 1,105 women who were about to have, or had just completed, an abortion, 24 percent considered the procedure to be morally wrong.[1] Based on the prevailing rate of 1 to 1.5 million abortions every year since 1974, the results of this study suggest that as many as 200,000 to 300,000 American women have seriously violated their own moral code every year for the past quarter century.

During the 1980s, hundreds of crisis pregnancy centers (CPCs) were founded throughout the United States by organizations seeking to provide meaningful alternatives to abortion. While CPCs focused their attention primarily upon the pregnant woman and her particular circumstances, nearly all of them unexpectedly found themselves working with another type of client: the woman with unresolved emotional issues arising from one or more abortions in the past— sometimes many years before. The centers were not beating the bushes to find women who were dealing with this pain, nor were they broadcasting guilt-inducing messages that would have created it artificially. Rather, just as I had found, women were seeking a safe place in which they could reveal what they'd experienced, explore its significance, and come to terms with it.

Post-Abortion Syndrome

While CPC volunteers and staff members were hearing about post-abortion pain on an informal basis, a number of counselors and psychologists became aware of the impact of abortion on the lives of some of their clients. In pursuing this issue, they swam against the professional tide that generally ignored or minimized the importance of the abortion experience.[2] Yet as these therapists accumulated more cases and compared notes with one another, they noticed some striking similarities in the symptoms described by many of these women (and, in some instances, those closest to them). The abortion did not appear to be merely a convenient scapegoat to divert attention from deeper conflicts or the obsessive subject of an untreated depression or the focus of guilt-ridden fundamentalism. Furthermore, contrary to the pronouncements of abortion providers and apologists, there appeared to be far more than a handful of women who were having this difficulty. Judging by the number of CPCs in which post-abortion support groups were forming, there were perhaps thousands, if not millions, of women for whom abortion had spelled relief only temporarily.[3]

Drs. Anne Speckhard, Vincent Rue, Arthur Shostack, and David Reardon were among the first researchers to organize and publish many of these observations. Eventually the term post-abortion syndrome (or PAS)[4] was coined to designate an ongoing difficulty in the following areas:

◆ Processing the fear, anger, sadness, and guilt surrounding the abortion experience;

171

◆ Grieving the loss of the baby; and
◆ Finding peace with oneself, the others involved in the abortion decision, and God.

While the woman who has had the abortion is usually the focus of attention, most therapists who deal with this problem acknowledge that *any* person involved in the abortion decision is a possible candidate for PAS. Speckhard and Rue[5] subsequently described a type of disturbance with a shorter duration (less than six months), which occurs within three months of the abortion. They suggested that this be called post-abortion distress (PAD). They also proposed that post-abortion Syndrome could be considered one form of a condition called post-traumatic stress disorder (or PTSD), in which a highly stressful event generates a variety of chronic symptoms later in life.

For a number of years, these researchers have attempted to convince professional organizations such as the American Psychiatric Association (APA) that post-abortion syndrome should be recognized as a formal diagnosis.[6] Their efforts thus far have been unsuccessful for a number of reasons.[7] First and foremost, the addition of *any* new diagnosis to the body of disorders recognized by the APA is typically a long process—especially if the topic is politically charged. Unfortunately, no professional organization (especially the APA) is immune from political pressure, especially from its own members. For example, the symptoms of post-traumatic stress disorder were first observed among soldiers returning from Vietnam. Some feel that the official recognition of this syndrome by the APA was delayed—twelve years overall—because this war was so intensely controversial in American politics and public life. Similarly, the pro-choice position is currently so firmly entrenched within the APA and other professional groups that any official acknowledgment of widespread emotional consequences of abortion would be a major uphill battle. This is troubling considering the fact that so many women each year are seeking help for resolution of the guilt, anger, and grief experienced after an abortion.

What Does the Research (Not) Say?

Another important reason for the lack of formal recognition of PAS has been the relative scarcity of adequate research on abortion's psychological after-effects. This is surprising, given the fact that abortion is the most common medical procedure performed on women in the United States. When I first reviewed the relevant medical and psychological literature in 1985, I was surprised and somewhat dismayed by this situation.

Unfortunately, the research dealing with post-abortion issues hasn't improved much since that time, for a number of reasons. First, it is very difficult to probe an experience about which women are reluctant to talk. Because of the extremely sensitive nature of the abortion decision, many women are not willing to participate in a study of their own experience with it, even if the survey is anonymous. In national fertility surveys, for example, the percentage of women who report having had an abortion is only half of what would be expected based on published abortion rates. The implication is that many women do not even want to admit that they have had an abortion, let alone review it in detail with a total stranger. Furthermore, when researchers attempt to use abortion clinic records to follow up on patients, they find that some women have given false information to safeguard their anonymity. And in at least one study,[8] physicians were asked to approve or disapprove the mailing of a questionnaire to their post-abortion patients, thus potentially eliminating women for whom the survey process might be too painful. As a result, those who have suffered the most in the wake of their abortion experience may not be included in a given study. One researcher summarized the problem by noting that women who are more likely to find the abortion experience stressful may be underrepresented in volunteer samples.[9]

Furthermore, much of the research published on post-abortion distress has been based on clinical impressions, questionnaires and/or interviews conducted *within a few weeks or months after the abortion.* Normally it is logical to question someone soon after the experience under investigation. But with abortion, the prevailing emotion during this period is usually *relief* that a decision has been made and the crisis pregnancy resolved. The emotional toll of an abortion often appears many years after the procedure, long after the questionnaires have been filled out and returned. In one study, over 70 percent of the respondents stated that they would have denied the existence of any reactions for an extended period of time after their abortion(s)—as long as ten or fifteen years in many cases.[10] One researcher has concluded that studies of the adverse psychological effects of abortion are deficient because they ignore the possibility that reactions will surface years later.[11] Another researcher has suggested that many women are actually unable to mourn the loss of a child at the time of an abortion, resulting in a delayed grief reaction.[12]

In addition, many studies of the emotional consequences of abortion have been inadequately or improperly designed. This problem has been noted by researchers who have looked at the big picture by reviewing multiple studies on this topic—a process known as a *meta-analysis*. For example, researchers reviewed sixty-one research studies published between 1966 and 1985 and found the studies had an abundance of "significant methodological shortcomings."[13] In 1987, four researchers evaluated a total of seventy-five studies of post-abortion women. They found inadequate sample sizes—that is, the study involved too few women to draw meaningful conclusions—in 95 percent of the articles. A substantial number of the studies contained seven or more deficiencies in their overall design. The researchers also identified an eye-opening pattern: the studies with the greatest methodological weaknesses were more likely to report that women experienced positive emotions following an abortion.[14]

Finally, abortion is a highly charged issue for patients, health care providers, lawmakers, and the public at large—including researchers. It is extremely unlikely that an investigator will not have a pre-existing opinion about the morality of abortion and its impact on our society. Whether conducting the research or evaluating it after publication, those who fervently oppose abortion as the taking of innocent life will find their convictions bolstered by studies suggesting that this procedure poses significant physical and emotional risks to women as well. Likewise, those who adamantly support a woman's unimpeded access to abortion are likely to feel vindicated if a study suggests that the procedure has a positive (or at least neutral) impact on her life. Researchers may openly describe themselves as pro-choice or pro-life, casting a suspicious shadow on their summaries and conclusions. Not surprisingly, accusations of research bias and lack of integrity are often voiced whenever re-

175

search appears to support one or the other side of the argument.

Almost every major review of the professional literature on the psychological effects of abortion has suggested that preconceived assumptions pose a significant barrier to high-quality research. Indeed, authors who have attempted to summarize the existing research on this subject have come up with wildly diverse conclusions—even when analyzing the same body of material. One of the earliest reviews concluded that deeply held personal convictions frequently seem to outweigh the importance of data, especially when conclusions are drawn.[15]

A revealing chapter in the book *Feminist Perspectives on Social Work and Human Sexuality* reviewed the existing professional literature on abortion and concluded that "the proportion of women who experience varying degrees of post-abortion stress ranges from less than 10 percent for possible psychiatric sequelae to 50 percent for feelings of unhappiness or troubled thoughts. . . . It is superfluous to ask whether patients experience guilt—it is axiomatic that they will."[16] But in the same article, the authors admitted that "there is a reluctance to call attention to negative consequences of abortion for fear of being seen as providing support to anti-abortion. . . . pressure groups."[17]

Just as the professional literature fails to come to a consensus regarding post-abortion distress, books for the general reader also present sharply conflicting opinions about this topic. To a large degree these have been driven by the underlying beliefs of their authors regarding abortion itself. Books written by pro-life authors have described individual post-abortion experiences of pain, regret, and subsequent healing, challenging the notion that abortion is a relatively benign procedure. Examples include *Helping Women Re-*

cover from Abortion, Real Choices, Will I Cry Tomorrow? and *Her Choice to Heal.*[18]

On the other hand, books with a pro-choice/pro-abortion orientation, such as the popular compendium for women, *Our Bodies, Ourselves,*[19] have consistently asserted that any psychological disturbance following abortion is likely to be minor and transient unless a woman is already mentally unbalanced. Some authors have attributed emotional turbulence after abortion to hormonal changes arising from the pregnancy, or even the strain of making the necessary arrangements for the abortion.[20]

A Surgeon General Enters the Debate

In 1987 President Ronald Reagan directed Surgeon General C. Everett Koop to review the medical and psychological risks of abortion. After studying the evidence submitted by those on both sides of the issue, Koop submitted a four-page letter to the president stating that "the health effects of abortion on women are not easily separated from the hotly debated social issues that surround the practice of abortion." His bottom line:

> I have concluded in my review of this issue that, at this time, the available scientific evidence about the psychological sequelae of abortion simply cannot support either the preconceived beliefs of those pro-life or of those pro-choice. . . . The data do not support the premise that abortion does or does not cause or contribute to psychological problems.[21]

While Dr. Koop did not draw any clear conclusion

about the psychological effects of abortion, he did acknowledge the possibility that symptoms could arise long after the procedure and that this phenomenon could create problems for those attempting to study them. In testimony before Congress on March 16, 1989, he stated that "there is no doubt about the fact that there are those people who do have severe psychological problems after abortion. . . . If you study abortion the way many people have and see how well women feel about their decision three months after the actual procedure, you can be very badly misled."[22]

Shortly after Dr. Koop's conclusions were publicized, the American Psychological Association appointed an expert panel to survey the current professional literature. The panel concluded that most women do not suffer lasting effects from abortion.[23] Brian Wilcox, director of public interest legislation for this organization, stated that "it's clear that the vast majority of women are not going to experience any significant problems. Millions of women are having abortions, and it appears to be a relatively benign procedure both medically and psychologically."[24] The certainty of his conclusion seems somewhat unwarranted, however, in light of his agreement with Koop that most of the studies surveyed were flawed scientifically.

The Primal Wound

As difficult as it may be to carry out high-quality research on the long-term effects of abortion, I wholeheartedly support ongoing efforts to do so, and hope to see more meaningful results in the future. In the meantime, an ever increasing number of women continue to seek relief for emotional pain arising from a past abortion, and they have become harder to ignore. Even abortion providers have recognized that at least some women need special counseling. However, their willingness to address this need has been hampered by a fear that doing so might be viewed as an acknowledgment of abortion's potential harm to women. For this and other reasons, such programs have been slow to develop. As a result, clinic workers continue to struggle with the problem of dealing with patients—both before and after the procedure—who are conflicted about their abortions.

Journaling Exercise: Created for Love

❖ ❖ ❖ ❖ ❖ ❖

Below are some names, titles, and descriptions of God. Circle the ones that seem right in describing the way you *feel* about God. Remember—this is based strictly on *feelings* and not on what you think you know on an intellectual level.

The Beginning and
   the End
You who love the
   people
Judge
Light of the world
King of the ages
Friend
Defender of widows
Forgiving God
Architect
Love
Majestic glory
A shelter in the storm
Strength of my heart
An ever present help
   in trouble
The One who saves
Spirit of fire

Fortress of salvation
You who hear prayer
Creator of heaven and
   earth
My hope
Sanctuary
A source of strength
Our advocate
Father
God my Savior
God of all comfort
God of hope
God of retribution
He who reveals his
   thoughts to man
I AM
Judge of all the earth
Lord our shield
Lord who heals you

Lord who strikes the blow
Jealous and avenging God
A refuge
Deliverer
One to be feared

The One who sustains
Shepherd
Sovereign Lord
Consuming fire
The Almighty
Exalted God
Eternal king

Using separate paper, answer the following questions:

What did you learn about your *feelings* regarding God based on what you circled?

Do your feelings match your intellectual understanding of the relationship you have with God?

If you were standing before God right now, could you describe your relationship with him by saying (in addition to "I obey, serve, worship, and fear you"), "I love you with all my heart and all my soul and all my mind and all my strength"? Why or why not?

If you had to use some kind of analogy to describe your relationship to God (e.g., commander-in-chief to private, commander-in-chief to general, sweet old man to innocent child, slave-driver to slave, benevolent master to slave, wise teacher to daydreaming student), what would it be? Think about this before you write, and be as creative as possible. Don't give the "correct" biblical answer; rather, say how you really feel.

Why did you choose this analogy?

What is it about your life experience (from earliest memories to the present) that has contributed to creating this view of how God relates to you?

What did you "learn" from your mom and from your dad (separately) about God? Not just what they taught with words, but what did they convey to you through their behavior?

Do you *feel*, as well as know, that God loves you?

Do you *feel*, as well as know, that God likes you?

What reasons would you give for feeling this way?

What percentage of the time does it feel like God initiates loving communication with you?

What percentage of the time do you initiate loving communication with God?

What did you learn from each of your parents about love?

Can you think of a time in your life when you knew, beyond the shadow of any doubt, that God was directly paying attention to you and trying to tell you he cares about you?

How do you know it was God?

The Bible uses the parent/child relationship more than any other to describe how God wants to relate to us. Describe the ideal, perfect parent.

How did your own parent(s) fall short of this ideal?

How did you think this might hinder you today in your ability to have a loving parent/child relationship with God?

As surely as a mother falls in love with her child as he/she emerges from the womb, God fell in love with you the moment he created you. Do you ever *feel* this?

What do you think is your biggest block to feeling God's love and approval of you?

What do you think it would take to overcome this block?

Who administered punishment/discipline in your home most of the time when you were growing up?

What was the usual outcome of a discipline/punishment (e.g., sullenness and resentment, restoration, talking the episode through, continued condemnation, etc.)?

What did you "learn" from each of your parents about discipline, punishment, and forgiveness?

After reflecting on all the above, write a letter to God on another sheet of paper expressing your feelings about your relationship with him and his relationship with you ("Dear God . . .").

Look up the following verses and write them out:

Deuteronomy 6:4-5	1 John 4:9-19
Matthew 22:37-38	Jeremiah 31:3
John 3:16	Hosea 11:4
John 14:21	John 6:44-45,65
Romans 8:35-39	Deuteronomy 39:6
1 John 3:16	John 15:16

Which verse(s) hit you the hardest, and why?

Describe your feelings during and after this journaling project.

What was the most important thing(s) you learned during this journaling project?

Appendix Three

Teens and Abortion

❖ ❖ ❖ ❖ ❖ ❖

Sixteen-year-old Sandy sat on my couch, sobbing and clutching the teddy bear that she had tenderly taken down from a bookshelf in my office. Since her abortion three months ago, her despondency had increased to the point that she expressed a wish to die. Her frantic parents had called for this first counseling appointment. I could tell they were frightened, and I could also see why.

"He said not to worry if I got pregnant, that we'd get married. He lied! He bolted the minute I found out. How could he do this to me? I don't understand! I hate him, my parents hate me, and I feel like my life is over, or should be. . . ."

For millennia, teenagers have given their parents a steady supply of sleepless nights over the issue of sexuality. Each generation's parents are convinced that their own tribulations vastly overshadow whatever grief *their* parents endured. But those who are rearing adolescents during the turn of the twenty-first century may be truly justified in claiming that the task of bringing their offspring to adulthood without a sexual misadventure—or catastrophe—is the most difficult in history. Today's teenagers are not only dealing with the usual quantities of broiling hormones and profound needs for love and affirmation. They are also making sexual decisions in a culture that is virtually driving them toward sexual experimentation, if not outright promiscuity.

It is hardly surprising that statistics regarding adolescent sexual behavior and its consequences tend to be uniformly discouraging:[1]

◆ By age eighteen, 56 percent of teen girls and 73 percent of teen boys have had intercourse.

◆ Every year 3 million teens acquire a sexually transmitted disease (STD).

◆ More than 1 million U.S. teens become pregnant annually—11 percent of *all* girls aged fifteen to nineteen. Of those, 36 percent decide to have an abortion.

◆ Only 61 percent of minors who have abortions do so with at least one parent's knowledge.

◆ By age twenty, more than four of every ten young women will have been pregnant.

◆ Nearly 20 percent of all pregnant, single teens will become pregnant again within a year.

◆ Less than 10 percent of the babies born to unmarried teens are placed in adoptive homes.

I have worked with hundreds of adolescents over the past fifteen years while directing or overseeing crisis pregnancy centers, and I continue to see them on a regular basis in my private practice. For a teen's parents, who often seem to have amnesia for their own teenage experiences, teens' moods and behavior can be exasperating—especially in sexual crisis situations. When dealing with a teenager who has experienced one or more abortions, a number of developmental and emotional issues complicate the landscape.

The powerful drive for autonomy apart from one's parents. The most important task of adolescence is to establish, over a period of several years, a viable and productive independence from one's parents. Although universal and inevitable, the process is rarely free of conflict. Most commonly, the adolescent's push for independence arrives well ahead of her parents' willingness to grant it—or, indeed, her capacity to manage its responsibilities.

In a best-case scenario, a smooth and healthy transition from childhood to adult independence occurs because the following are in place:

◇ A solid home "port" from which to venture. A teenager who has been consistently cherished and affirmed in a stable environment is usually better equipped to tackle new challenges with confidence, competence, and a healthy regard for consequences.

◇ A stable level of communication with her parent or parents, who are gradually (and deliberately) releasing their control and authority over an extended period of time. This process of "working themselves out of a job" requires both timeworn wisdom and artful improvisation.

Unfortunately, in many families these ingredients are in short supply. As half of all marriages end in divorce, too many children will experience the upheaval of a family break-up. Some parents who have been embroiled in conflict for years mistakenly believe that they can finally go their separate ways because the kids can "handle it now that they're older." A father's role in his daughter's life, which is particularly important during her early adolescent years (eleven to fifteen), may be permanently altered (or effectively ended) during the course of separation, divorce, and remarriage. All too often, a teen may find her home breaking apart at the very time she most needs stability. I have often cringed as a couple in therapy calmly considers a divorce when there is a young adolescent at home. While divorce almost always has a detrimental effect on children, it is especially devastating for a young teen.

If parents' lives are in turmoil, healthy communications will likely be crippled. Parents may be too preoccupied with their own crises to be able to seize the opportunities when a teen is willing to talk. Communication can also be stifled if the parents do not understand that the process of "pulling away" is a natural part of every teenager's life. In addition, the teen may be too angry, upset, or withdrawn because of her parents' conflicts to attempt meaningful conversation with them.

Even if her parents aren't in conflict, the passage to adulthood may be stormy. Her declarations of independence may be interpreted (correctly or otherwise) as articles of war, pulling the parental reins even tighter. Seeing only dismal restrictions on the horizon, the teen may feel more misunderstood and less willing to explain her point of view. ("They're hopeless. Why bother?") She may generalize this belief to all adults, an important issue if she is meeting with a counselor, doctor, pastor, or other caregiver in a crisis situation.

The need to establish her own identity. Between the ages of three and early adolescence, children are usually content to adopt their parents' value system. This may come to an end by age twelve or thirteen, a shock to unprepared parents. A once-compliant daughter may suddenly demonstrate behaviors and express opinions that are out of step with the family party line. Experiments in appearance—clothes, hairstyle and color, earrings, and other body hardware—

may be tried on with abandon. Music emanating from her stereo may make her bedroom resemble a pulsating boiler room, with lyrics that (if understandable) sound hardly uplifting. Parental wisdom and insight that was heeded throughout childhood may be suddenly tossed aside in favor of the half-baked opinions of a classmate she met last week. Parents who are unprepared—or have only dim recollections of their own adolescence—may be uncomfortable, if not downright alarmed, by this exploration process.

This is a time for cool heads to prevail and for learning the art of choosing battles carefully. Some issues, such as alcohol use, illicit drug use, and premarital sex, must be addressed fervently because of their far-reaching (and at times life-threatening) consequences. Other issues with less profound implications, such as clothing choice or hairstyle, can be addressed with healthy reality checks. This often means the daughter experiences the consequences of her choices, within safe reason. Unfortunately, many parents hamper their daughter's maturing process by reacting with equal dismay to every situation, whether it is a messy room or the discovery of condoms in that room. The teenager concludes that reasonable communication with her parent(s) is hopeless because all she hears is an endless stream of negatives.

During the ongoing struggle to define her identity, a teenager is likely to be more preoccupied with herself than at any other time in her life. This self-absorption often makes it difficult for her to be sensitive to (or even acknowledge) the pain or viewpoint of others. She may seem appropriately described as "selfish." However, it is important for the adults in her life to understand that this deficit is nearly always temporary. It is likely the product of struggle and confusion rather than malicious intent. At this stage she may seem to flip between childlike thinking one day and adult comprehension the next, a pattern that can be exasperating for those who are trying to help her work through a crisis.

Issues for a Teenager Facing a Crisis Pregancy

In addition to the pressures an adult woman confronts when experiencing a crisis pregnancy, teenagers face other issues.

The decision to continue her pregnancy or to have an abortion is often controlled by parents, peer group, or boyfriend. It is difficult for teens to take personal responsibility for their decisions. The pregnant teenager tends to look for external sources to reflect back to her the theories she is trying on about herself. As a result she is strongly influenced by the opinions of others and is likely to see the abortion decision as externally determined.

Parents: If the girl's parents know about the pregnancy, the daughter is likely to go along with their opinion about what should be done. Most teens seeking a pregnancy test will tell the counselor or doctor, "My parents will *kill* me if they find out I'm pregnant." While this is usually a gross overstatement, it is important not to discount or trivialize this fear. The counselor or physician needs to take the time to inquire about her family situation. It is also crucial to help her "script" how she will tell her parent(s), and to follow up with her closely in the days after the appointment.

I first met Melinda when she came one evening to the Crisis Pregnancy Center where I worked. She wanted a pregnancy test, she was sixteen, and she was terribly frightened. She came from a Christian home and was the apple of her daddy's eye. Her pregnancy test was positive. She had good communication with her parents but was paralyzed by the thought of telling them that she had even had sex, much less that she was now pregnant. She told me there was no good out for her in this situation except to have an abortion, a procedure she considered morally wrong. She tearfully explained that she could not face her parents' bitter disappointment at the news of a pregnancy.

After talking for an hour or so, it was apparent that Melinda could not consent to an abortion. I asked her if she would like me to call her parents and invite them to join us, since it might be better for her to break the news in a safe place. I warned her that her parents' reaction would most likely pass through several stages, beginning with anger, and that it might take several days for them to accept the fact of her pregnancy.

When Melinda's parents heard where I was calling from, there was a dead silence on the other end of the line, and then a curt "we'll be right there." When they arrived, I took them into my office first and, with Melinda's permission, gave them the bad news. Melinda's mom began crying and her father's face hardened like stone. For a half hour, I took the first wave of their shock and anger, so that by the time Melinda meekly came into the room, they had had a little time to adjust to the information. Mom hugged her tightly, but Dad couldn't even look at her. I explained to the family that it would take several days to assimilate this turn that their lives had taken, and cautioned Melinda not to expect her parents to be terribly supportive for a few days. I urged them to resist the urge to make any immediate decisions.

By the time I saw the family the following week, a tentative peace had been reached between Melinda and her parents. Mom and Dad continued through a predictable grieving process for several weeks. By the time the baby's kicks could be felt by "Grandpa," he was beginning to look forward to the birth.

Peers: The impact of peers on an adolescent cannot be overstated. Their approval is extremely important, more so than at any other time of the girl's life. If her peers have accepted at least one other single pregnant girl carrying the baby to term, this will have a profound effect on a pregnant teenager's decision. I counseled with one girl who decided to have an abortion because her friends told her she was an idiot to ruin her figure when bikini weather was right around the corner. Not long after, I counseled another girl who decided to carry her baby to term because she thought it was "so cool" that her pregnant friend had received so much attention at school. Public opinion is a powerful force in high school!

Boyfriend: The relationship with a boyfriend can drive the decision to abort or carry. For the past two or three decades, men have been hearing a message that they should not express (or even *have*) an opinion on this issue but should simply support whatever the woman wants to do with their unplanned pregnancy. In my experience, however, if a teenage boy is invited to explore and verbalize his feelings about this situation, he will express strong opinions about what his girlfriend should do. Typically communication skills are not this highly developed in teen relationships. As a result, it is not uncommon for a young man, confused and frightened about his role in the situation, to clam up and even withdraw emotional support from his girlfriend, leaving her to feel unsupported. A woman who feels abandoned by the father of her baby will often decide to have an abortion.

Fifteen-year-old Susan and her boyfriend Sean came to the Crisis Pregnancy Center for a test. Their behavior was typical for young clients: they were nervous, they held hands, and they did not speak much with one another. I first took Susan into the counseling office by herself, where she mournfully told me the age-old story of fumbling sexual exploration leading to unprotected intercourse. The test was positive, and I asked if she had any thoughts about what she would do.

"I don't know," she sobbed. "I guess I'll have to have an abortion." I asked her if Sean had offered any opinions about the issue. He had already told her that if she became pregnant, the decision would be up to her, and he would pay for an abortion if that was what she wanted.

"But what does Sean *hope* you will do?"

Susan looked bewildered. "I'm not sure," she countered.

"Well, why don't we bring him in and ask him?" I suggested.

It turned out that Sean did, indeed, have an opinion but didn't feel he had the right to verbalize it. He thought Susan should be free to make a decision by herself. When I pressed him to speak his feelings, he hesitantly said that he wished Susan would carry their baby.

"But why didn't you *tell* me?" asked a stunned Susan. "I would have had an abortion because I thought that's what you wanted me to do."

"Why would you think that's what I wanted?"

"Because you never said you wanted me to keep it!"

"Well, you're the one who has to go through the pregnancy. I can't tell you what to do!"

The abortion decision can be greatly influenced by the availability of this procedure. Pregnant teenagers tend to opt for abortion more often when it is readily available in their community, when public funding is obtainable, and when confidentiality is ensured. Depending upon their developmental and emotional maturity, they may be less interested in thoughtfully weighing their options than in getting out of some very hot water. Solutions that offer a quick and quiet way out of the crisis are very tempting. Also, despite whatever trendy cynicism they might express about the world of adults and their institutions, I have discovered that teens can have a remarkable and surprisingly naïve trust in the system. I've lost count of the number of adolescent girls who have looked me squarely in the eye and said, "If abortion was dangerous at all, it wouldn't be legal."

Concerns about her physical body. A girl in her mid-adolescent years (ages fourteen to seventeen) is in the process of intense physical changes. She is likely to be very concerned, if not highly insecure, about her body—how it looks and functions, whether she likes it (or anyone else does), and how she should treat it. A pregnancy multiplies these concerns because it will inevitably bring about its own profound physical changes. This change on top of change may be more than she can bear—or thinks she can bear—adding to the crisis and an intense desire for a speedy conclusion.

Issues for Teenagers Who Have Had an Abortion

The teen who has had an abortion may have different

concerns than a woman who has had an abortion after the teen years.

The abortion is a relatively recent event. A woman who is distressed over a recent abortion is in a very different place from one who has suppressed the painful emotions involved in an abortion in the distant past. For a teenager who has had an abortion, the wounds are likely to be fresh, intense, and immediate.

I generally try to meet with a post-abortion teen one-on-one rather than in a group setting. Her primary emotion is probably anger. Working with her individually, it is possible to provide a safe place for her to discharge explosive feelings. If she cannot talk through these negative emotions, she may become depressed and even suicidal. Meeting with a counselor who will accept her unconditionally may give her (and those around her) some breathing room until she is ready to work through her struggles.

Many teens have lost hope that they might meet an adult who will listen to them without responding with a lecture or reprimand. It is a powerful gift for a teenager to receive permission simply to express her feelings without being told how she *ought* to feel.

It is often difficult for a teen to separate the loss of the baby from the loss of the boyfriend. Very often, the breakup with her boyfriend—which may have been her first "serious" relationship—occurs shortly before or after an abortion. The decision to abort may have been an irrational attempt to punish a boyfriend who was pulling away. Or, she may have scheduled the abortion with the mistaken belief that this would return the relationship to its former glory. It is important for her to grieve each loss individually.

It is unfortunate that many grown women (especially those with teenage daughters!) have forgotten how desperately in love a sixteen-year-old girl can feel. While I believe that an adolescent rarely (if ever) has the emotional maturity to enter into a stable marriage, I never discount the intensity of a teenager's attachment to the object of her affection. An adolescent girl may give herself sexually to her first serious boyfriend because she naïvely (but genuinely) believes they are at the beginning of a long relationship. If she has been unexpectedly dumped after having an abortion—especially if this was her first "true love" or her first sexual experience—the rejection and betrayal she feels can be devastating.

The post-abortion teen is more likely to have another abortion than a woman who had an abortion as a mature adult. In a study involving more than 31,000 New York teenagers, those who had one prior abortion were found to be four to six times more likely to terminate a subsequent pregnancy than those who had never had an abortion. There are a number of possible reasons for this:

◆ A desperate desire for love and acceptance (especially if the teenager has been abandoned by the father of the baby she aborted), possibly combined with a reduced resistance to sexual overtures.
◆ The "damaged goods" syndrome. She's had sex, perhaps with a number of partners, and now an abortion as well. Why hold out if someone wants sex now? Without a significant reorientation of values, and a rebuilding of self-concept, there may not be any compelling reason to save her sexuality for a future husband.

◆ A chaotic lifestyle, including destructive relationships, drug and/or alcohol abuse, and unwillingness to take measures to prevent pregnancy.

◆ In some cases, an unconscious (or even conscious) desire to create a replacement for the
baby she has lost, even when her circumstances
are no more favorable for rearing a child. Some
teenagers have a very idealized notion of what
caring for a baby is like, believing it is similar to
bringing home a puppy from the pet store or
even a new doll from the toy shop. If she has
been part of a chaotic family system and feels
abandoned by Mom and Dad, a baby can represent the chance to start over with a new family.
She may assume that the baby will love her unconditionally and that she will find immediate
fulfillment in her role as a new mother. This
wistful longing often intensifies in the weeks and
months following an abortion. If she does indeed
become pregnant again, however, the same pressures that drove her to have the previous abortion are likely to be present again.

**The post-abortion teen is more likely than an older
post-abortion woman to think about suicide.** I believe
that she is a higher suicide risk because:

◆ She is less able than an older woman to deny
the humanity of the baby.

◆ She is likely to have made the abortion decision
with more secrecy than an older woman, and
thus has less support afterward.

◆ She is likely to be grieving the loss of her boyfriend as well as the baby.

◆ Teenagers are prone to feel their losses more
deeply than they will later in life.

◆ A teen's coping skills are less developed than they will be during adulthood.

Talitha's Story

Very early in my counseling career, I nearly made a fatal mistake with a client. Talitha, eighteen, came into our Crisis Pregnancy Center on one particularly busy day in early January. She wanted a pregnancy test, and because all of the other staff and volunteers were helping clients I talked with her and took care of the test myself. The test was positive, and Talitha left intending to have an abortion in order to appease her boyfriend. It seemed obvious to me that Talitha did not really want to have an abortion, but nothing I could say about the fragile loyalty of boyfriends would change her mind. I gave her a hug and encouraged her to call me at the Center if she ever needed to talk in the future.

In late February, a very hysterical Talitha did indeed call. She had had the abortion shortly after our conversation. Now several weeks later she was still extremely upset. After she arrived in my office, she wept for an entire hour. Her boyfriend had left her two weeks after the abortion, and the two girlfriends who had urged her to end her pregnancy no longer wanted to hear about it. Her mother had supported the abortion decision but was now emotionally withdrawn. Talitha was furious with everyone. After a fierce ventilation of her feelings she felt a little better, and we made another appointment.

The following week was a repeat of the first session. In fact, a long series of appointments followed over the next several months, each one virtually duplicating that first hour of tears and bitter anger. I gently tried to move her toward addressing her situation, but she resisted my efforts.

By April I was growing weary of what appeared to be a regular waste of an hour for both of us. But while I had not yet received formal training regarding the grieving process, something told me that it was important to keep going. And so with a box of tissue in hand, I met her with honest compassion each week, holding her and listening to the same passionate litany. She was barely holding on to her job and had isolated herself from former friends and family members who didn't know about the abortion.

Finally, late in May, something changed. Talitha arrived in my office wearing makeup for the first time, and no tears flowed over it during our session. To my amazement (and relief), she asked if I had a workbook in which she could journal her thoughts. I gave her a post-abortion workbook, and she returned the following week having worked through the first two chapters.

Over the next three months we worked through the rest of the book. Talitha made wonderful progress in her overall outlook, forgiveness of herself and others involved in the abortion decision, and grief over the loss of her child. She even experienced a spiritual renewal. Her smile was genuine and unclouded.

In early September Talitha announced that she was going to attend college out of state. I was truly sad to know that our weekly meetings would soon be ending. I had developed a real affection for Talitha over our six-month journey. At our last meeting, she made this astonishing statement: "Teri, I want to thank you for being willing to hold me and listen to me for all of those months when I couldn't do anything but talk about how angry I was. I'm not stupid. I know it must have been hard for you to meet with me week after week when I wasn't making any progress. But I want you to know something: You were the only person in my life who was willing to listen to my pain. Believe it or not, I was actually thinking about killing myself if you had decided to stop listening to me, like everyone else did. Thank you for being there for me."

One of the most amazing gifts of adolescence is the ability to *feel* one's experiences fully and deeply. As we grow older, we may learn to modulate our feelings to a more manageable level. Sometimes, we make an unconscious decision to stop feeling altogether (if, for some reason, feelings have become dangerous). But a teenager usually has not accumulated enough life experiences to make these adjustments, to understand how the world operates, and—most importantly—to learn that she can survive and thrive even after difficult or devastating experiences. The emotional complexities of a crisis pregnancy and a subsequent abortion should never be underestimated.

Appendix Four

More for Friends, Men, Family, and Pastors

❖ ❖ ❖ ❖ ❖ ❖

Whenever I speak or teach on the issue of healing after an abortion, I know that those in the audience have come for a variety of reasons. Most are professional or lay counselors who want to learn how to help a woman cope with the emotional aftereffects of her abortion. But there are always a number of people who come because abortion has personally affected them or someone close to them and they are seeking to understand their own pain.

Similarly, I know that this book will be perused by those seeking to help post-abortion women as well as by those seeking information for themselves or someone they love. I would like to speak on a more personal level to those specific groups of readers.

If You Have a Friend Who Had an Abortion

I have never spoken to a group about abortion without at least one person coming up to me afterward and saying something like: "I have a friend who had an abortion a few years ago, and so much of what you say sounds just like her story. But when I've tried bringing it up, she made it clear she didn't want to talk about it. After listening to you, I understand now that she must be in denial. How can I help her?"

Here's the bottom line: You cannot break someone's denial. It is the very nature of denial that the more you try to talk with another about an uncomfortable issue—one that the other doesn't want to deal with—the more the other will resist your effort. The only exception to this rule is a carefully planned event known as an *intervention*, in which close friends and family, preferably under the guidance of a professional therapist, confront an alcoholic or a drug addict. This is a technique intended to lead a person directly into intensive therapy and is most certainly *not* one I would recommend, under any circumstances, for a post-abortion woman.

If a woman is denying the negative emotions related to an abortion, she has probably created a fragile balance: she has learned to function adequately by locking away that episode of her life into a recess of her mind where it is not integrated into the normal, everyday flow of her conscious thoughts. As a result, if you try to talk about it, you pose a major threat to the system she has worked out for herself.

If the other person is a good friend, with whom no subject has been off-limits before, you might feel hurt that she would want to withhold this experience from you. I believe we *all* have carefully—perhaps desperately—guarded secrets that cause the pulse to quicken and the face to flush when we think about them or imagine someone else discovering them. If we have never forgiven ourselves for those choices, we will feel shame and regret.

If you have never had an abortion yourself, it may be incredibly difficult for you to understand how disconsolate your friend feels. Your approach may communicate a caring, nonjudgmental attitude: "All right, so you made a mistake. We *all* make mistakes in our lives. I'm not going to judge you! If you talk about it for a while, you'll feel so much better. What's the big deal?" But your friend may hear what you say as: "All right, so you murdered your own child. We all make mistakes!" If this is how she sees her abortion choice, there is nothing you can say that will help minimize her self-condemnation. Even worse, she may have told someone previously and received a judgmental response. When that happens, she learns that it is *not* safe to tell anyone.

So what can you do? If you do not have a close history with this friend, you probably don't have enough of a foundation to approach the issue of a previous abortion. Your best approach in this case is to be sensitive when you are around her. For example, should the general topic come up in a social gathering, take care that whatever you say about post-abortion women is measured and sympathetic. You may even have to take a defensive stand if someone in your circle of friends speaks in a judgmental way about women who have had abortions.

On the other hand, if you *do* have a longstanding and intimate relationship with her, you can approach the issue of a previous abortion—provided that you are willing to back off immediately if she is not receptive. You might start out by saying something like, "I know I brought this up before and didn't do a very good job of it. I want to apologize for that. And if you still don't want to talk about it, I'll respect that." Then, rather than *telling* her why you think she is suffering from post-abortion stress, just ask questions.

Often when I am in therapy with a client, the answer to what's going on with her seems so obvious that it hangs between us like a giant neon sign. Everything in me wants to shortcut the process by simply explaining to her what I see. But I have learned, over the years, that if I spoon-feed the answer to a client, she will not internalize it. She must have that Aha! experience herself, and it can only come when someone is willing to explore her experience in a supportive, nonjudgmental way, typically through asking good questions. The healing process often begins with a trusted friend whose response says, "You are no less worthy in my opinion because of what you just told me."

If you are not willing to have a mutually self-disclosing relationship with a friend, don't bother trying to educate her about post-abortion syndrome. Very early in my training, I heard a familiar phrase that has always stayed with me: No one cares what you know until they know that you care.

If You Are a Man Who Has Been Involved in an Abortion Choice

Our culture's recognition of the need for women to grieve after an abortion is woefully deficient. Recognition of the need for men to grieve is virtually nonexistent. I can count on one hand the number of organizations that specifically address the reaction of men to abortion.

One reason post-abortion women are finally beginning to receive the help they need is that women are more likely to seek assistance for emotional issues. In the majority of marital counseling cases, it is the wife who makes the initial phone call. Her husband generally will join her only when he is facing a choice between counseling and losing her. Many times I have heard a husband say something such as, "No offense, but I am very uncomfortable with this whole thing. I don't agree with airing our dirty laundry with a total stranger."

If you are a man reading this book, you are most likely dealing with one of the following situations:

- Your girlfriend/wife had an abortion against your wishes.
- Your girlfriend/wife had an abortion and you didn't take a position one way or the other.
- You pressured your girlfriend/wife into having an abortion against her desires.
- Your girlfriend/wife had an abortion without your knowledge.

It is my opinion that men deal with many of the same issues that post-abortion women face. In addition, I think that a serious underlying issue for many men dealing with a wife's or girlfriend's abortion is a feeling of lost masculinity.

Many men still have a traditional sense of masculinity defined in terms of the power, right, and duty to protect and provide for his family. But because he has no legal say in the outcome of his girlfriend's or wife's pregnancy (in most states), the woman's right to make a unilateral decision to end the life of his child can create feelings of utter helplessness and even rage. A man's instinct to protect his family is stripped away. He may have trouble trusting women. He may experience guilt before God for not fulfilling his role as father-protector. If he instigated the abortion decision, he may feel guilty about the physical or emotional pain that his partner has suffered since the procedure. If he pressured his partner into having an abortion, the chances are high that he has since lost the relationship, and he may be utterly bewildered as to what happened. All of this can contribute to a profound sense of failure as a man.

If any of this sounds familiar, I would urge you

to consider beginning a healing process by contacting Fathers & Brothers for further information and help.[1] Also *Healing a Father's Heart,* by Linda Cochrane and Kathy Jones, is a study written specifically for men.[2]

If You Are the Parents of a Post-Abortion Woman

You may have arranged for your young daughter to have an abortion many years ago and were firmly convinced that you were acting in her best interests. Or perhaps you found out about your daughter's abortion long afterward, and it broke your heart. In either case, a painful gulf may exist between you and your daughter, and the abortion has become a topic that is carefully avoided. You may not know how to approach this issue with your daughter if you haven't yet resolved your own anger, grief, and guilt. Occasionally some old questions may return with a vengeance:

- Did I do the right thing when I insisted that she have an abortion?
- Has she ever forgiven me?
- Why didn't she tell us that she was pregnant, and give us the chance to help her? Why did she go through that experience by herself?
- How could she destroy my grandchild?
- How did I fail as a parent?

In my experience, most parents raise a daughter to be sexually chaste. If they don't expect their daughter to be a virgin on her wedding night, they at least expect her to be careful. So when a teenage girl announces with fear and trembling that she's pregnant, her parents inevitably take it as a personal failure, an *F* on their parenting report card. It is humiliating to think about the awkward and judgmental reactions of friends and family when they hear the embarrassing news. All of the carefully laid plans and cherished dreams for their daughter are now threatened by a few moments of runaway hormones. Needless to say, most parents are extremely unhappy about the prospect of dealing with this situation. The abortion is scheduled and the daughter's tears ignored—not because the parent hates her but because the parent loves her and believes this to be the best solution to ensure her future happiness.

The grief comes at some point after the abortion because this was, after all, a grandchild, whether the parent had a vote in the abortion decision or not. But there is no vehicle for mourning this loss. As years roll by, every bad choice made by the daughter gives a guilty nudge to the parent who wonders if the abortion was the right thing to do.

If you pressured your daughter into having an abortion years ago, you might want to consider approaching her and asking for forgiveness. If she is well into her adult years, and especially if she has a teenage daughter herself, she is probably in a position to understand that your motivation was to do what appeared to be the best thing for her at the time. Be prepared, however, to hear how angry and bitter your early decision made her and what it has cost her since that time.

If you have learned about the abortion months or years after it occurred, you may feel angry that your daughter made such an important decision without seeking your input or support. I would suggest that you find a way to deal with this anger before you approach her. It is likely that she already carries a heavy load of self-hatred and she doesn't need your additional vote. Once you have worked through your own anger, you may be able to initiate a time of healing in your relationship. The suggestions at the beginning of this appendix regarding a friend's approach to a post-abortion woman are applicable here as well. Tell her how grieved you are that she faced this crisis alone and that you don't condemn her.

If You Are a Pastor

I have often been amazed by the number of the clergy who naïvely believe that few, if any, women in their congregation have had an abortion. Surveys have repeatedly demonstrated that the percentage of churchgoing women who have had abortions is the same as among the population at large.

Sadly, few pastors are willing to address the abortion issue at all. If an annual address is given on the topic, there is little if any compassion extended to the post-abortion woman. I have often listened to a woman lament that she will avoid attending any service dealing with the issue because of the condemnation that she feels.

While some of this is the product of her own guilt, there is an element of truth to her perception. If the church has taken a pro-life stand, the Sanctity of Life Sunday sermon will usually focus on education and opportunities for political action. Rarely will there be compassionate recognition of the sizable percentage of post-abortion women sitting in the congregation. I have had many women tell me that after a pro-life sermon they often overhear comments such as, "How could a woman kill her own child?" Instead of walking away with a message of hope and reconciliation, the post-abortion woman frequently slinks out of a church service with the firm conviction that this is not a safe place to divulge her secret.

A tool I highly recommend to the clergy is a little book called *The Jericho Plan*,[3] which is an excellent resource for suggested sermon outlines addressing the emotional needs of the post-abortion woman.

If you are a member of the clergy, you are the representative of God to those who sit in your congregation. The post-abortion woman will form her understanding of God's view of her experience largely based upon your attitude and words. She needs to hear from you that God readily extends forgiveness to the penitent. Above all, she needs to be reconciled to God, and to experience his—and your—blessing.

Appendix Five

Proposed Diagnostic Criteria for Post-Abortion Syndrome

❖ ❖ ❖ ❖ ❖ ❖

At this time, post-abortion stress is not officially acknowledged by the professional community as a psychological disorder. If it were, PAS would be recognized in the Diagnostic and Statistical Manual (DSM).[1]

Those of us who do therapy with post-abortion women hope that PAS will one day be widely acknowledged. To this end, the following is a diagnostic description of PAS as it might appear in the DSM[2]:

Diagnostic Criteria A

An event that is beyond the range of usual human experience and is psychologically traumatic.

Diagnostic Criteria B: Event re-experienced

1. intrusive, spontaneous thoughts and images triggered by sounds, sights, smells
2. nightmares
3. flashbacks; actually like being back in the situation
4. distress when reading/seeing abortion related articles, shows, etc.; can last for seconds or weeks or months
5. common triggers:
   ◆ subsequent pregnancy
   ◆ being around babies/children

  ◆ being around pregnant women
  ◆ vacuum cleaners
  ◆ medical offices/clinics
  ◆ doctor's offices
  ◆ Mother's Day
6. anniversary reaction:
  ◆ date of abortion
  ◆ date of imminent delivery
  ◆ needling, uncomfortable feeling; feeling a bit crazy on date of abortion or imminent delivery

Diagnostic Criteria C: Avoidance and/or numbing of general responsiveness

  ◆ fear/protection of the emotional pain of facing the abortion

Diagnostic Criteria D: Symptoms

1. use of defense mechanisms in response to abortion memories *very often* characterized by substance abuse
  ◆ sex
  ◆ drugs
  ◆ alcohol
2. avoidance behaviors
  ◆ avoids children/families, e.g. shopping at midnight to avoid seeing children/families, avoids church because of family element/children
  ◆ isolates from family/friends
3. emotional and behavioral responses
  ◆ numbing
  ◆ low self-esteem
  ◆ depression; majority were suicidal at some point
  ◆ symptoms of depression

✦ sleep disorders
✦ change in hunger patterns
✦ very painful thoughts
✦ feel very hopeless
✦ lethargy, listlessness, and at same time have inner anxiety
✦ crying for no reason
❖ guilt
❖ frequent crying

4. anxiety manifesting itself in psychosomatic symptoms (real physical symptoms due to psychological factors)
   ❖ sleep disorders
   ❖ abdominal pain
   ❖ cervical pain and often pain during intercourse
   ❖ eating disorders

5. self-punishing or self-degrading behaviors
   ❖ promiscuity
   ❖ pattern of entering abusive relationships
   ❖ self-abusive: small percentage anorexic, cutting, hitting self
   ❖ fear of going into doctor's office, fear of doctor

6. preoccupation with the aborted child
   ❖ may perceive visitations from child, usually perceived as angry or hurt child
   ❖ compulsive imagining of what child would look like or be like
   ❖ can lead to anniversary reactions and second pregnancy

7. system consequences: troubled relationships
   ❖ opposite sex: anger toward actual man involved with abortion, when not dealt with, is transferred into a new relationship
   ❖ children
     ✦ often most vulnerable with child immedi-

ately following abortion
- ✧ child is replacement child; child has to be perfect
- ✧ if wanted child was a girl but child is a boy, bonding may not take place
- ✧ overprotection (have to protect them and keep them alive; need to help them; ultimately they can't control their life/death)
- ◆ family
  - ✧ may pull back from family: isolate; everyone may know something is wrong but no one will talk
  - ✧ can become divisive: alliance with one family member; tells one but not the other

Appendix Six

Suggested Resources

❖ ❖ ❖ ❖ ❖ ❖

Training Manuals

◆ The *Post-Abortion Counseling Trainer's Manual* ($40 U.S., $55 Canadian) and the accompanying *Peer Counselor's Training Manual* ($20 U.S., $30 Canadian) may be ordered in the U.S. from Teri Reisser, 1885 Montgomery Road, Thousand Oaks, CA 91360 (805-379-9606), and in Canada from Angie Côté 5077 59A St., Delta, B.C., Canada V4K 3K1 (604-946-4628). Please add $5.00 shipping for first manual and $2.00 for each manual thereafter.

Post-Abortion Studies

◆ *Forgiven and Set Free* by Linda Cochrane. Grand Rapids: Baker, 1986.
◆ *Healing a Father's Heart* by Linda Cochrane and Kathy Jones is specifically written for post-abortion men. Grand Rapids: Baker, 1986.
◆ *A Season to Heal* by Penny Salazar-Phillips and Luci Freed is an excellent tool for someone not desiring a Christian study. Order from: Alternatives Pregnancy Center, 1860 Larimer St., #200, Denver, CO 80202, (303-298-8815) or through Cumberland House (615-832-1171).
◆ *Our Healing Journey*, produced by the Diocese of Lansing, is an excellent study for Catholic

women. Order from: Project Rachel, 1500 E. Saginaw St., Lansing, MI 48906-5550.

Books

◆ *Aborted Women: Silent No More* by David Reardon. Westchester, IL: Crossway, 1987.
◆ *Does Anyone Feel Like I Do?* by Pam Koerbel. New York: Bantam Doubleday Dell, 1990.
◆ *Help for the Post-Abortion Woman* by Teri Reisser and Paul Reisser. Lewiston, NY: LifeCycle Books, 1994.
◆ *Helping Women Recover from Abortion* by Nancy Michels. Minneapolis: Bethany House, 1988.
◆ *Her Choice to Heal* by Sydna Massé and Joan Phillips. Colorado Springs: Chariot Victor, 1998.
◆ *The Jericho Plan: Breaking Down the Walls Which Prevent Post-Abortion Healing* by David Reardon is an excellent book to give to pastors to educate them about post-abortion issues. Includes sample sermons on the subject. Springfield, IL: Acorn Books, 1996.
◆ *Mommy, Please Don't Cry* by Linda DeYmaz. Sisters, OR: Questar, 1996.
◆ *Real Choices* by Frederica Mathewes-Green. Ben Lomond, CA: Conciliar Press, 1994.
◆ *Will I Cry Tomorrow?* by Susan Stanford. Grand Rapids: Fleming Revell, 1986.

Men and Abortion

◆ *Men and Abortion: A Path to Healing* by C. T. Coyle. Belleville, Ontario, Canada: Essence, 1999.
◆ *Men and Abortion* by Arthur Shostak and Gary McLouth. Praeger: 1984.
◆ Fathers & Brothers Ministries, 350 Broadway #40, Boulder, CO 80303; (303) 494-3282.

Research Sources

◆ Dr. Vincent Rue, Institute for Pregnancy Loss, 111 Bow St., Portsmouth, NH 03801-3838; (603) 431-1904. Ask for a list of materials to order.

◆ *Research Bulletin.* To subscribe, contact Association for Interdisciplinary Research in Values and Social Change, 419 7th St., NW, #500, Washington, D.C. 20004.

◆ *The Post-Abortion Review.* To subscribe, contact The Elliott Institute, P.O. Box 7348, Springfield, IL 62791-7348.

National Training Conference

◆ CareNet, 109 Carpenter Dr., #100, Sterling, VA 20164, (703) 478-5661. This conference offers a preconference that covers basic post-abortion counselor training. In addition, there is a track just for men.

National Post-Abortion Organizations

◆ The Elliott Institute, P.O. Box 7348, Springfield, IL 62791-7348.

◆ National Office of Post-Abortion Reconciliation and Healing (NOPARH), P.O. Box 07477, Milwaukee, WI 53207-0477; (414) 483-4141 or (800) WECARE.

◆ Post-Abortion Counseling and Education (PACE), 109 Carpenter Dr., #100, Sterling, VA 20164; (703) 478-5661.

◆ Ramah International, 1050 Galley Square, Colorado Springs, CO 80915.

Miscellaneous

◆ National Memorial for the Unborn, 6230 Vance

Rd., Chattanooga, TN 37421; (423) 954-9552 or (800) 505-5565. For a small donation, an individual can have a name plaque added to a permanent marble wall.

Notes

❖ ❖ ❖ ❖ ❖ ❖

Chapter One: The Experience No One Talks About

1. "Abortion Surveillance: Preliminary Analysis—United States, 1996," *Morbidity and Mortality Weekly Report,* Centers for Disease Control, Vol. 47., 4 Dec. 1998.

2. Steven Waldman, Elise Ackerman, and Rita Rubin, "Abortions in America," *U.S. News and World Report,* 19 Jan. 1998, 20.

3. As quoted in Frederica Mathewes-Green, *Real Choices* (Ben Lomond, CA: Conciliar Press, 1994), 11.

4. Ibid.

Chapter Two: No Longer Coping

1. Colman McCarthy, "The Real Anguish of Abortions," *Washington Post,* 48, 5 Feb. 1989.

2. With rare exception, those who are emotionally distraught and worried that they are "going insane" are in fact not. Ironically, individuals who are developing a true psychosis (a biochemically mediated thought disorder that causes a literal break from reality) are typically highly resistant to the suggestion that they have a problem, psychiatric or otherwise.

3. "Trends in Adolescent Pregnancy and Childbearing," Office of Population Affairs website, *www.hhs.gov/progorg/opa*

4. David Reardon, *A Survey of Psychological Reactions* (Springfield, IL: Elliot Institute, 1987).

5. M. Gissler et al. "Suicides After Pregnancy in Finland, 1987-94: Register Linkage Study," *British Medical Journal* 313:1431, 7 Dec. 1996.

6. American Association of Suicidology website, *www.suicidology.org/suicide.htm*

7. Philip G. Ney, "Induced Abortion and Its Relationship to Child Abuse and Neglect," *Association for Interdisciplinary Research in Values and Social Change Newsletter,* 4:1, Spring 1991.

8. Laboring on behalf of one side or the other in the pro-life/pro-choice controversy might seem like a logical path to follow, but this is usually not the healthiest arena for a woman with unresolved emotions from an abortion. An exception might be a crisis pregnancy center in which a counselor who is familiar with post-abortion issues can identify and help resolve those struggles or steer her toward a post-abortion support group.

9. "New Study Confirms Link Between Abortion and Substance Abuse," *The Post-Abortion Review*, 1:3, Fall 1993.

10. M. T. Mandelson et al., "Low Birth Weight in Relation to Multiple Induced Abortions," *American Journal of Public Health* 82(3):391, March 1992.

Chapter Five: Guilt and Forgiveness

1. The content of this chapter is oriented primarily toward women with this cultural background. Of course, women from a different cultural/religious background would not necessarily deal with spiritual issues in the same way.

2. Two excellent books that review the various ways in which people view God are *Your God Is Too Small* by J. B. Phillips (New York: Macmillan, 1987) and *The Father Heart of God* by Floyd McClung, Jr. (Eugene, OR: Harvest House, 1985).

Chapter Six: Releasing the Anger

1. Linda Cochrane, *Forgiven and Set Free* (Grand Rapids: Baker, 1986).

2. Women who come into a post-abortion group often express frustration and anger when their husband/boyfriend does not support their attending the group. If he was the father of the aborted baby, he may have his own post-abortion issues. He may resent the fact that his wife/girlfriend is "stirring the pot" again by deliberately focusing on an episode he would prefer to be forgotten. If he was *not* the father of the aborted baby, he may feel resentful that she wants to spend time in a group where she will be discussing her prior sexual relationship with another man.

Chapter Seven: Accepting the Loss

1. Ally Sheedy, *Yesterday I Saw the Sun* (New York: Summit Books, 1991).

2. If a local clergy member is invited to officiate at the ceremony, it will probably be a "first" for him or her. It is crucial that *specific* direction be given regarding the part he or she will play, along with an explanation of the issues that have been explored during therapy (guilt, anger, and grief). A sermon on the morality of abortion is absolutely *not* what is needed for this service. But pastoral presence is important because it provides a visual representation of God's acceptance of the women. A brief (ten-minute at most) message of encouragement and reconciliation is most appropriate, ending with a blessing of the women. Ideas for topics include (1) our children have died, and we give those children dignity by remembering them at this service; (2) God understands our grief and pain; (3) God cares for the unborn; (4) God wants us to go on with our lives.

Chapter Eight: Moving On

1. Because this can be an emotionally charged subject, when it appears appropriate—and only with the woman's consent—I send home a letter explaining to him why she has come to counseling or a post-abortion group, what the therapy or group work will be covering, and how he can best support her as she works through her healing journey.

Appendix One: A Brief History of Post-Abortion Syndrome

1. David R. Zimmerman (1987), "Abortion Clinics' Toughest Cases," *Medical World News*, 55-61.
2. R. Mester (1978), "Induced Abortion in Psychotherapy," *Psychotherapy and Psychosomatics*, 30, 98-104.
3. During a 1988 radio talk show, I broached this issue with the medical director of Planned Parenthood in Los Angeles. Without missing a beat, she stated that, out of the 1.5 million women who would have an abortion that year in the United States, only a hundred or so would experience any significant emotional distress in the wake of this procedure. I countered that if her statistics were correct, it was an amazing coincidence that nearly all of these women happened to live in my hometown. In the previous three years, I had worked in depth with well over one hundred women (in a community of about 100,000) who had experienced major difficulties arising from a past abortion.

4. Some authors use the term "post-abortion stress," abbreviated PAS, to identify this problem.

5. A. Speckhard and V. Rue (1993), "Complicated Mourning: Dynamics of Impacted Post-Abortion Grief." *Pre- and Perinatal Psychology Journal*, 8(1), 5-32.

6. A proposed diagnostic description of PAS is included as appendix 5.

7. At one point abortion was listed as a "psychosocial stressor" in the third edition of the APA's *Diagnostic and Statistical Manual* (DSM-III-R), a book that serves as the reference standard for therapists in the United States. (American Psychiatric Association: *Diagnostic and Statistical Manual of Mental Disorders*, Third Edition, Revised [DSM-III-R]. Washington, D.C., American Psychiatric Association, 1987, p. 20.) However, it was not listed as an example in the newest revision (the DSM-IV) published in 1994.

8. K. R. Niswander and R. Patterson (1967), "Psychological Reaction to Therapeutic Abortion." *American Journal of Obstetrics and Gynecology*, 114, 29-33.

9. E. Adler et al. (1990), "Psychological Responses After Abortion," *Science*, 41-44.

10. D. Reardon, *Aborted Women: Silent No More* (Westchester, IL: Crossway, 1987).

11. M. Gibbons (1984), "Psychiatric Sequelae of Induced Abortion," *Journal of the Royal College of General Practitioners*, 34, 146-150.

12. Mattinson, J. (1985), "The Effect of Abortion on a Marriage," *Ciba Foundation Symposium*. 115, 165-177.

13. J. Lyons et al. (1988), "Research on the Psychological Impact of Abortion: Systematic Review of the Literature 1966 to 1985," from an unpublished paper prepared for Family Research Council, Washington, D.C.

14. V. Rue et al. (1987). "The Psychological Aftermath of Abortion: A White Paper," presented to Surgeon General C. Everett Koop, commenting on the 1967 Niswander and Patterson study.

15. N. M. Simon and A.G. Senturia, A.G. (1966), "Psychiatric Sequelae of Abortion: Review of the Literature: 1935-1964, *Archives of General Psychiatry*, 15, 378-389.

16. K. Lodl, A. McGettigan, and J. Bucy (1985), "Women's Responses to Abortion: Implications for Post-Abortion Support Groups," *Feminist Perspectives on Social Work and Human Sexuality*, 3, 119-132.

17. Ibid.

18. Susan Stanford, *Will I Cry Tomorrow?* (Grand Rapids: Fleming Revell, 1986); Nancy Michels, *Helping Women Recover from Abortion* (Minneapolis: Bethany House, 1988); Frederica Mathewes-Green, *Real Choices* (Ben Lomond, CA: Conciliar Press, 1994); Sydna Massé and Joan Phillips *Her Choice to Heal* (Colorado Springs, CO: Chariot Victor, 1998).

19. Boston Women's Health Book Collective, *Our Bodies, Ourselves for the New Century: A Book by and for Women* (n.c.: Touchstone, 1998).

20. For example, one self-help book entitled *A Woman's Guide to Safe Abortion* (Maria Corsaro and Carole Korzeniowsky [New York: Holt, Rinehart and Winston, 1983] 47, 58) states that:

> Many women feel slightly "down" after the abortion. This may be connected with the hormonal change. If you've felt this sort of thing before, during your monthly ovulation or menstruation, then you know what we mean. Added to that, of course, is the strain of rushing around to arrange for tests and the abortion, and the physical stress of the operation itself. So if you feel a little weepy and shaky, it's very understandable.

21. C. Everett Koop (1989a, January 9). "Letter to President Reagan," in *Medical and Psychological Impact of Abortion*, pp. 68-71. (Washington, DC: U.S. Printing Office).

22. C. Everett Koop (1989b, March 16), "Testimony before the Human Resources and Intergovernmental Relations Subcommittee of the Committee on Government Operations, House of Representatives," in *Medical and Psychological Impact of Abortion*. Washington, DC: U.S. Printing Office, 232 and 241.

23. Adler, E. et al (October 1992), "Psychological Factors in Abortion: A Review," *American Psychologist*, 1194-1204.

24. Wilcox (1989), "Study: Abortion Harm," *Los Angeles Times*.

Appendix Three: Teens and Abortion

1. "Pregnancy and Childbearing Among U.S. Teens," Fact Sheet, Planned Parenthood Association of America, Inc., June 1993.

www.plannedparenthood.org/library/TEEN-PREGNANCY/childbearing.htm

Appendix Four: More for Friends, Men, Family, and Pastors

1. Fathers & Brothers Ministries, 350 Broadway #40, Boulder, CO 80303; (303) 494-3282.

2. Linda Cochrane and Kathy Jones, *Healing a Father's Heart* (Grand Rapids: Baker, 1986).

3. David Reardon, *The Jericho Plan* (Springfield, IL: Acorn Books, 1996).

Appendix Five: Proposed Diagnostic Criteria for Post-Abortion Syndrome

1. The DSM is a compendium of officially recognized counseling issues. The criteria for publication in this manual is based on widely accepted and reproducible research. The professional counseling community recognizes this manual as the final authority of counseling issues.

2. This material was taught by Linda Ross at the PACE Institute in Phoenix, Arizona, 1990. It follows closely the criteria for PAS proposed by Dr. Vincent Rue. Criterion classifications correspond to those of Posttraumatic Stress Disorder (PTSD).